: y
u

'u.

IN A FEW WORDS
GET RID OF THE LOG

KEN SCOTT

2022

ISBN 978-1-387-83543-0
Imprint: Lulu.com

DEDICATION

I wish to dedicate this short book to my family, beginning with my wife Jeannie, the love of my life. I include Rebecca, our daughter and her husband Ganesh, and their delightful children, Anjali, and Ajay. Our son Samuel and his wife Deborah complete that immediate circle.

MATTHEW 7:1-5

"[1] Do not judge others, and you will not be judged. [2] For you will be treated as you treat others. The standard you use in judging is the standard by which you will be judged. [3] And why worry about a speck in your friend's eye when you have a log in your own? [4] How can you think about saying to your friend, 'Let me help you get rid of that speck in your eye, when you can't see past the log in your own eye?' [5] Hypocrite! **First get rid of the log in your own eye;** *then you will see well enough to deal with the speck in your friend's eye."*

ACKNOWLEDGEMENTS

This is the fourth English language book to be authored by me during what is called the Covid-19 pandemic. I owe it in large part to the personal space gained during the lockdowns and to the change in social contacts for its completion. It was time for me to turn my attention to put in writing several issues of personal faith, rather than continuing to produce tomes, in Spanish, of a more academic nature.

There are too many people to thank for my experiences in life. My late parents are high on the list for communicating their faith in Christ to me. Orcadian culture was surely formative. My wife Jeannie has shared over 47 years of her life with me and is part of so much contained in this book's pages. My own family, children, grandchildren, siblings, relatives, friends, work colleagues, pastors, mission directors, and so many more, have had a hand to play in the lines and between the lines of what I write.

When I add in the role that the individuals in the Kirkwall Baptist Church, Regions Beyond Missionary Union, Latin Link, Belfast Bible College, Newtownbreda Baptist Church, Baptist Missions, the Irish Baptist College, St Patrick's Drumbeg Church of Ireland, and those in Peruvian and American churches have contributed towards the enrichment of life, I trust I have not forgotten to acknowledge anyone. I thank God for you all.

My thanks to Alistair, my youngest brother, who prepared yet another manuscript for publishing. As always, I take full responsibility for the content of the book and for all limitations contained in it.

ENDORSEMENTS

In a Few Words. Get Rid of the Log - is the account of one man's journey where we see his desire to walk closely with his God and his continual battle with *"the logs"* that are intent on making that walk as challenging as possible. The author's autobiographical style presents the biblical call to reflect Christ in all that we are and do, in a way that enables the reader to identify closely with the challenges.

There is an adage that states – *"you never really know a person until you have lived with them."* Having worked and travelled with Ken on several occasions as we missioned together in Peru I can attest to that statement. The account of his early years and experiences *"explain a lot."* These have clearly shaped the person we know.

The book's honesty makes it both an uncomfortable and an encouraging read. As Ken works through *"the logs"* the reader cannot escape the fact that these and similar *"logs"* are faced by everyone who seeks to live a godly life. The prayers at the end of each section provide helpful personal responses to make this a very profitable read.

I commend this book along with every other tool that aids us in our pursuit of our likeness to Christ, to be seized and applied in our daily quest to truly reflect that image.

> **Pastor Alan Baird, long-term pastor of several Baptist churches, lecturer in the Irish Baptist College, and three times President of the Association of Baptist Churches in Ireland.**

Ken writes with a freshness and honesty, reflecting on the experiences of his life from childhood to *"getting older."* He reviews life through the lens of family and ministry. There is an endearing humility in how this book has been written, as Ken does not shy away from admitting how lessons have had to be learned along the way. He juxtaposes his personal vulnerability and sure-footedness in faith. This is a candid critique of ministry life, laying bare regret around how family so easily comes second to the mission God had called us into and offering wisdom for those with ears to hear. Ken looks back and invites us to learn from his life and to fully live in step with the Spirit, whilst laying bare and slaying for us some of the foolish practices in the life and ministry of God's church.

In this narrative we meet a man who has discovered the beauty of Christian faith in all its diversity, making for a genuine and emotionally rewarding read. He underlines that fellowship with the saved in Christ Jesus is so much more important than the secondary doctrinal differences which cause division. There is a call to unity in Christ running through the whole narrative.

I commend this as a refreshing read which willingly confronts some of the *"hot potatoes"* of the Church. In this book there is much to learn from the real-life pilgrimage of one of God's children. We would expect nothing less from an Orcadian who has been touched by the Spirit of the living God!

Rev Willie Nixon, Rector of St Patrick's Church of Ireland, Drumbeg

Apollos was all the richer because he had met Priscilla and Aquila. They opened their home and the way of God more fully to him, and no doubt to many others. Now, in this book Ken opens the realities of a missionary family home while also exploring and explaining the way of his Lord more adequately in very personal and practical terms. It is written out of a lifetime of experience. It is pointedly personal, practical yet never *"preachy."* Against the background of so much Christian literature this is gritty rather than glitzy. Ken's pen recounts the reflections of a man who can now look back in real terms of a long obedience in the same direction since childhood.

Rev Desi Maxwell, Minister of Presbyterian Church in Ireland, preacher, lecturer, conference speaker, with local and international ministries in Xplorations.

Ken Scott, in dealing with some of the *"logs"* that have obscured his spiritual vision, allows the readers to see into his heart. It is an extremely open and honest reflection on who he is. He seeks to show how his family background, his personality, his personal experiences and opportunities in life and in Christian service and, above all, by the grace of God have, and still are, contributing to the process of making him who he will yet be. I believe that the writing of this book has been a blessing to Ken, and I am sure it will be a real blessing to the readers as they identify with many of the *"logs"* in their own eyes, so encouraging and enabling them not only to clear their vision but to press on towards the point when God will complete his work in them.

Rev Robin Quinn, Minister of Presbyterian Church in Ireland, missionary in Africa.

The author is a proud Orcadian, which for the uninitiated is a native of the Orkney Islands that lie to the far north of Scotland. I have been privileged to know Ken and his wife Jeannie since the 1980s, when we met through a mutual involvement with a mission agency working in Peru.

In this book the author shares his heart about some areas of his own life where he has struggled to live out a kingdom lifestyle. You will recognise some, if not many of them, from your own experience as they are *"logs"* which are common to many of us who endeavour to live out the life of Christ.

Ken gives an unvarnished account of family dynamics and his early life experiences in Orkney. He describes the way in which they either strengthened him for his future life journey or rather created reactions within him which he has had to learn to leave behind by the help of the Word and the Spirit.

In a Few Words. Get Rid of the Log - is a book that will provide help and hope to all who may think they are the only ones who struggle with the *"logs"* described here or the many other *"logs"* which may be recalled as you read.

Rev David Craig, recently retired from pastoring Bournemouth Community Church. Rev Craig continues to minister in local and international mission.

The opening chapter of this book has transported me back fifty years. I made some wonderful visits to Orkney, staying with the Scott family on their farm. Since then, my friend, Ken Scott, has travelled many miles and experienced numerous adventures in his service for the Lord Jesus Christ. This book, *"In a Few Words,"* will give you a glimpse into the mind and heart of Ken. The honesty and humility that comes through these pages, were clearly forged in the home of his godly parents.

Mention of the inner pharisee, anger, and getting older may prove to be uncomfortable reading as they will certainly make you face up to your real self. I particularly enjoyed reading the prayers at the conclusion of each chapter, they blessed me immensely.

This book must be recommended for every person going into full time Christian service. There are many books on *"how to succeed"* in ministry, but very few on dealing with issues of the heart, and our true motives in the promotion of the Gospel. Buy this book, it will help you re-evaluate your Christian walk, then make sure that others benefit from it as well.

Rev Allan Penduck, Minister of Assemblies of God for forty years in Worcester, Newport South Wales, and in Gornal/Dudley. Allan has ministered in North America, eastern Europe, and in India. Allan was a magistrate and family court judge for twenty-six years.

My intention in this book is to write *"in a few words"* about matters that I have called the *"logs"* that needed attention. I suspect I am not alone in this. Sadly, I have observed that even very well-educated people do not read very much. I acknowledge that as a reason for my attempt to be brief. I have included more than I first intended but still hope that that I might coax some into a little bedtime reading, otherwise those who are able to read possess no advantage over those who cannot read.

I cannot remember a time in my life that I did not believe in the existence of God. Childhood understanding of the atoning sacrifice of Jesus Christ on the cross set me on my journey of life. Was it not Jesus who claimed to be *"the way, the truth, and the life"* and that *"no one can come to the Father except"* through him (John 14:6)?

In my earliest attempts to study the Bible and to pray I began a search for all the pieces in this jigsaw. The quest to experience Jesus on life's journey has frequently been an effort to weigh up the many-faceted nature of God to be relevant, at the same time hard-hitting, and yet caring.

I became a Christian at ten years of age. Since then and for over the last sixty years I have been learning what it means to belong to God, to love Jesus, and my neighbour. What concerns me as I seek to grow in my relationship with God is how that might work itself out daily. The exercise of seeking to be entirely honest with myself is, I believe, a wise one. Regarding a daily walk with the Lord, the best victory is to self-conquer.

That is basically what this book is about. My intention is neither to be overly academic nor to present theological arguments for my beliefs but simply to recount a list of personal issues I have had to rework. I freely acknowledge that while I have lived my life with the intention of meeting the spiritual needs of others, I have been more blinkered than I at first realized.

The world in which we grow up is undoubtedly the main starting place for our understanding of our God-given spot on the earth. It is therefore the contributing part to be examined by the Spirit of God. The following chapters represent a select catalogue of issues. They are personal to me, and I have evaluated the list several times with a view to changing it. As I did so I removed six of my original themes that I deemed did not fit in. Those that remain are just some of the reasons why I continue to be a work in progress in God's hands.

INTRODUCTION

Three memories remain with me from my pre-school years. The first is of me playing contentedly in the building sand on the family farm with my metallic Dinky tractor and trailer. The fact that another use was made of the sand by several cats did not dissuade me. Anyway, that probably built-up antibodies at such a young age. It seemed those happy days would never end.

The second recollection is of when I spent an afternoon playing by myself in an imaginary world under some iron girders that leaned against a stone dyke. From within my vantage point, I was aware that Father was up the road busily engaged in chores alongside the farm workers. It was only as I returned home that I discovered Father had also seen me. He smiled, commenting that he had noticed me *"hard at work."* What bliss!

My third memory related to my desire for some hobnail boots and a kilt. I was fascinated by both. I loved the noise that, what we called, in Orkney, the *"tackety boots"* made when the farm employees walked on solid surfaces. As to the kilt, I had seen men use them at the agricultural shows. Both were for men and boys like me. Each time I knew that Father was off to Kirkwall on farm business I asked him to get me some boots and a kilt. I was always keen to find him as soon as he returned. He came back empty handed, but he assured me that *"next time"* he would get them. My hope stayed alive.

My idyllic pre-school existence changed when I began to attend the Harray Public School in 1954 at five years of age. I remember that I was the only boy in the class alongside three girls. That was fine, but I was jolted into another level of existence in my second year. My oldest brother Tom, who completed P 7 during my P 1 year, had moved on to the Stromness Academy some miles away. It was my first day in P 2, as I was sheltering under a wall in the playground, when several boys from P 7 grabbed me and gave me a stark choice. They asked me whether I wanted them to give me a thrashing or whether they should give it to my brother Robert, by then in P 6. I only hesitated long enough for those giants to start in on me until I succumbed to the blackmail. I cried out, *"Robert! Robert!"* It was a hellish year for Robert.

Both Robert and I were traumatized, he with bruises, and me with guilt and fear. Once that year had passed and Robert was in P 7, peace returned. It was after he left for Stromness Academy that things heated up. Trouble had been brewing for my older brother Ivan, two years above me, and he and a classmate – we will call him *"the boxer"* as his father had taught him his boxing skills – had their regular skirmishes. I was aware that I was smaller and skinnier than two bullies from the class below me. They were both bigger than me and knew it. Looking over my shoulder became normal from then on. The fights for survival increased and more than once I was saved by the bell.

Before I left the Harray Public School I was determined to make amends for what had happened to Robert and Ivan. So it was that I waited one day for *"the boxer."* I remember it well. After all, he was always fighting with Ivan, so he had it coming! The best I could do was hit him across the chin as he passed by innocently. He flew one way, and I ran the other. When he caught me, I got the thrashing of my life. It felt great!

One cold day while sheltering under the school stone dyke one of *"my"* two bullies dropped a huge stone on my head from the other side. As I was coming to, it took me a while to understand why I felt warm sticky liquid running down my face. After being patched up by the headmaster's wife, my father collected me and took me to the doctor's surgery so that a stitch or two could be applied.

My strategy changed after that. It seemed to me that instead of waiting to be attacked, often simultaneously from both sides, I needed to single out each *"enemy,"* in isolation the one from the other, and go in, without warning, with fists flying. Two battles ensued, and, for the most part, the war was over.

Away from the classroom it was back home to life in an ever-increasing family [1]. Father had always seen to it that we older boys had chores on the farm. In my last two years in Primary School, he used to collect me after classes so that I could accompany him in his long wheel-based Land Rover piled up with silage. He owned land some seven miles away. My task was to drive slowly along the tracks while Father forked out the silage to the cattle he wintered outdoors.

Only once, tired, and hungry, when father was not already waiting for me, did I attempt to run home across some fields to escape, but was caught in the act. That cost me dearly and Father never arrived late

---

[1] The final list of siblings, complete with middle names: Thomas Mowat [26-03-43], Robert Eunson [24-05-45], Ivan Rendall [13-11-46], Kenneth David [30-01-49], Doreen Bertha [22-02-52], James Martin [10-08-55], George Reid [05-06-58], and Alistair Drever [09-11-63].

again! Meanwhile, Doreen, three years younger than me, had to walk home over a mile and a half in the opposite direction in the cold and ensuing darkness.

To my knowledge my parents were oblivious to much of what went on at school. I thought it was a normal part of growing up. On another level, it was a family routine to attend church on Sunday. I recall being puzzled by fellow-pupils who argued that all religions might be true, and not just the Christian faith. I imagine they had heard that elsewhere. That seemed silly to me as alternative realities could not all be true. While I acknowledged that all could be false, I was convinced that Jesus Christ was "*the way, the truth and the life*" [John 14:6].

We were given pocket money as children on a weekly basis. I seem to remember that I was awarded a shilling each week. There were twenty shillings in a pound and the smallest paper money was the ten-shilling note. We were encouraged to save up our money for our annual holidays on the northern islands of Stronsay and Westray. My practice was to exchange my coins for paper money as soon as I could. I will never forget finding mother's purse one day and giving in to temptation by taking two shillings. My mistake was to then ask mother to exchange my coins for the coveted ten shillings.

I had not counted on Mother's memory nor on her obsession for numbers and statistics. After a private and public grilling that finally led to confession and punishment, Mother convinced me that I needed to sort my life out. I was ten, and cannot think of all she said, but do remember, among other things, a mention of hell. That aside, I did not need to be convinced in my conscience that what I wanted was to tell the Lord all that I knew about myself and to give myself to all that I understood of Jesus Christ. I accepted I was guilty before God and that Jesus' death on the cross could bring me into a relationship with him. Thus, I prayed for forgiveness and asked Jesus into my life.

Instantaneous sainthood did not follow! I am sure that my siblings and others would attest to that. One major change was that I never knowingly took what did not belong to me again in my life. I also consciously prayed more and asked the Lord to enable me to avoid fights. As I consider this, my final two years in Primary School were relatively peaceful. More of that in a later chapter.

It was during my second traumatic year at school that I decided to ease the pressure on myself and not finish my work in class. While I suffered continuous reprimands from the teacher, no other serious consequences followed. Academic laziness developed into a pattern. The Eleven-Plus examinations in my final year would determine whether I followed my three older brothers to Stromness Academy or to a Community School. I knew by that stage that I needed the Lord's help, so I asked him to aid me. Imagine my relief when I passed! I still claim that to be a miracle.

I trace my respect for my older brothers to those formative years, my dislike of bullies, the ability to survive by constantly looking over my shoulder, and my resorting to aggressive action when *"necessary."* I guess I was also up for a fight back then. Diplomacy was a much later addition! Some early entrenched tendencies have been difficult to overcome.

It was one thing to yield my life to God and quite another to learn to live each moment of each day in fellowship with the Lord. Growing into a fuller experience of God is what this book is about, and of seeking to remove obstacles from the path. This is my journey of living for Christ and of humbling myself enough to clearly identify some of *"the logs"* in my life that hindered me from seeing God plainly, hearing him distinctly, and following him daily.

PRAYER

Heavenly Father, we ask that you give us wise minds and spirits, attuned to your will, and so acquire a thorough understanding of the ways in which you work. Help us each one to live well for you Lord and thus to please you. Teach us to learn more of how you work and thus to be trained to do your work. We pray that you will give us the strength to stick it out over the long haul through the power you give. Make it a force that endures the intolerable and that always spills over into joy. Amen

CHAPTER 1   FAMILY BACKGROUND

One of my favourite BBC television programmes is *"Who do you think you are?"* The idea appears to be to highlight how different celebrities study their lineages and family trees, usually learning surprising secrets they never knew about their families. Documentation of birth, census, marriage, property, court cases, along with death certificates of ancestors are analysed to emphasize the role that family history plays in a specific celebrity's daily life.

The stories are often poignant and emotional as they come to know of personal struggles. The resulting hour-long broadcasts educate about life as it used to be where children died of diseases that are easily prevented today. Prejudice, previously accepted as the norm, co-existed with a lack of social safety nets, in a world that invariably led to destitution.

The inquiries remind me of how far we have come in some respects. It has been opt-repeated that *"those who fail to learn from history are doomed to repeat it."* While this is true at many levels, I am convinced that if we do not know where we came from, it is difficult to know where we are going.

There is a proverb in English that declares *"experience is the best teacher."* Given that proverbs are just that - wise sayings – that have a context within which to be applied, the experiences of life lead everyone to live out their existence within a specific worldview. A brief definition enables a clearer understanding:

> *A worldview is the way in which we view or consider the world. It is a set of presuppositions, or assumptions, which we hold, consciously or unconsciously, about the basic make-up of our world.*

I suppose an even simpler way of expressing this is to understand what makes us tick.

Life has passed very quickly, and my wife Jeannie and I often muse about how rich and varied our experiences have been. She first met my parents at the airport in Orkney in August of 1978, almost four years after our marriage in the United States on the 28th of December 1974, more than three years after us living in Peru as a couple, and when Jeannie was eight months pregnant with our second child, Samuel.

To state that she suffered culture shock as she came to terms with *"my world"* would be true.

THE EUNSONS

After doing some research into my ancestry on my mother's side of the family[2] I discovered that my grandfather, Robert Eunson (1887-1974), married Isabella Drever (1889-1965) on the island of Westray in 1910. Before I was born in 1949, my Eunson grandparents had already lost four of their thirteen children. Margaret Eunson died soon after she was born in 1910, Thomas (Tommy - 1922-1932) drowned before his tenth birthday, Christina (Chrissie – 1924-1928) was taken by a childhood disease, and another Margaret (Maggy), died aged 32 in 1948. The youngest, Uncle Frank (1934-2021), was the last of the siblings to die, aged 86.

Grandfather Eunson lived most of his life on the Island of Westray in Orkney. I remember him as a larger-than-life character who frequently spoke his mind. The last time I saw him alive was before I left Orkney in early 1973, headed for Latin America. He reminisced more about his life than usual. For years he had emphasized, as Orcadians used to do, with a certain pride, the aging process by claiming an extra year. He would say something like, *"I am eighty years of age comes next year."* Grandfather Eunson had served in the First World War as a groom, with the task of looking after horses. As a soldier he manned a machinegun. Like many others from that era, he never spoke of whether he had killed men as he strafed enemy locations with bullets.

He was wounded twice. Once he was gassed and as a result was hospitalized and again when he was shot in the thigh by a bullet. For some reason, on that, my final visit, he felt compelled to show me the wounds. He remembered that rations in the trenches were sparse for conscripted soldiers. He explained: *"Some days just a piece of bread and tea made by boiling water from around your feet."* The great thing about going to the hospital, he told me, with a twinkle in his eye, was that he gained weight. He had ended up just *"like skin and bone and was down to ten stones and eight pounds."* I remembered him always as a large, big-boned Viking. He continued:

---

[2] I acknowledge a debt to my brother Alistair, the genealogist in the family, for sending me family trees for grandfathers Robert Eunson and Thomas Scott. My brother Ivan sent me a typescript on *"Eunsons in Westray"* and an obituary for my great-grandfather John Scott. Besides, I consulted various books detailing some family histories in Orkney.

The time I was gassed, the damage to me was just on my legs, and they stuck together. The man in the next bed had suffered stomach damage from the gas. He could not eat, even if he had wanted to, so he offered his food to me. I was eating for two and gained three stones in weight in just a few weeks, before they sent me back to the trenches.

He told me the same story that several in my extended family will remember. He related the fact that one day while tending his horse, he heard a voice telling him to move to the other side. No sooner had he done so than the horse was shot dead by a German bullet at the very place where he had been standing. He was a man of faith in God and always believed the Lord had given the warning and saved his life. If he had died on that battlefield I, and several hundred Orcadians, spread over succeeding generations, would never have been born[3].

We may never know how much Grandfather Eunson was shaped by his experiences in the First World War. What I particularly remember of him from my boyhood is that he held very strong opinions. He attributed value to hard physical work. Once, when waiting for the boat to take my brother Ivan and me back to Kirkwall, I remember him speaking loudly about someone we will call John for convenience: *"Look at him, John who has never done a day's work in his life."*

Grandfather's way of doing things was right! On one occasion, he related to Isabella (Granny Eunson), on return from a walk down the hill to the village of Pierowall how he had seen how a certain *"stupid"* man had hitched up his horse to the cart. Granny, a jollier and much gentler soul, replied that she hoped he had not said anything to the man. The reply: *"No, but I unhitched the horse and did it properly."*

My grandfather bore in his large hands the evidence of having worked too hard from a young age and until his dying days. Repetitive action, after using a sledgehammer to break building stones, he claimed, caused the muscles on both hands between thumb and index finger to completely waste away. In common with him the same muscle wastage happened on my right hand. That is another story.

With the benefit of hindsight, I acknowledge my mother to have been like him in several character traits. The Eunson genes were evident in

---

[3] The above recollections of my grandfather are also recorded in my book, *Anecdotes of an Orcadian. To Peru and Back,* July 2020, 11-12.

others of her siblings but that is not for me to share here. Mother was born Catherine Eunson in Braehead, my grandparents' stone-built cottage on the island of Westray, in March 1920. She was the middle child of a total of thirteen siblings. Grandfather laboured his entire life to be the breadwinner, in employment, by keeping laying hens, and in tending his vegetable garden.

Highlights of the year were holidays in Westray where we boys enjoyed Grandfather's fresh free-range eggs for breakfast with real locally made farmhouse butter on our toast. His new potatoes graced the table for lunch. The outhouse with old newspapers instead of toilet rolls was novel. Days ended when the lamps were lit in the evenings. In early years we travelled there with mother. As a strict disciplinarian she made sure that older brother Ivan was restrained by force from running about on the ferry until he had no more strength to resist. Emancipation had arrived when we were allowed to travel to Westray and back by ourselves. Such memories!

There is little doubt in my mind that my mother was a chip off the old block! Memories of Westray and of Grandfather Eunson echo in her! She raised her eight children as best she could and always did what she considered to be right. Her sense of right and wrong was absolute, and she certainly believed that a good *"singer[4]"* on the leg, or even on the *"side of the head"* solved misdemeanours. When too harassed or frustrated she handed me over to father on three occasions. Ah, now, there I do have painful recollections.

Well, those were different times! I still muse, with a mixture of mischief, awe, reflection, and pleasure, of several highlights which I wish to share. These illustrate mother's worldview, that is, of what made her tick. She would speak nostalgically of her memories of Westray and recounted the strange accents on the island, especially of those in Skelwick, just a mile or two away to the south from where she was brought up. It did not seem to occur to her that her Westray accent might sound weird with her liberal inclusion of *"thee"* and *"thoo[5]."*

Mother's understanding of dialects was common in Orkney. Orcadians often made fun of other *"weird"* accents on the islands. This came home to me when I returned after spending five years in South America. Jeannie and I were speaking to one of my cousins in Kirkwall, when her

---

[4] Mother's Orcadian word for a slap.
[5] Meaning *"you."*

husband, born and bred in Westray, blurted out in disgust to me, *"Fir goodness sake min spaek right [6]."*

Similarly, when meeting another married-in member of the family for the first time, that person, with equal disdain, blurted out to those present as he laughed, *"he spaeks just like Jonathan."* Jonathan is my nephew who studied medicine away and now lives in the USA. These were good conversation-stoppers! Orcadians refer to *"proper spoken"* people as those from outside who speak English without a hint of dialect. Mother is to be lauded for recognising a diversity of accents, except her own!

Anyway, enough detour! Mother kept a little red notebook in which she recorded our school grades, and vital statistics such as height and weight of all her children at different ages. I freely admit that my marks did not match up to those of my older three brothers and I was the smallest, along with Doreen, at age twelve. We each measured just four foot seven and a half inches. I weighed in at five and a half stone or 77 pounds at that stage of development. I am pleased to have ended up the third tallest sibling behind Ivan and our family giant, George. When I was about fifteen years of age, I came across that notebook quite by accident. I was sorely tempted to burn it but resisted the temptation. Brother George now owns that precious memento.

As Mother grew older her distinctive opinions came into their own and were voiced liberally when she sat in her armchair. It was when she would notice such supposed physical features in someone in public that I did ask her on occasion to refrain from speaking. If that was unsuccessful, which it normally was, then I would ask her to at least turn down the volume. It was her right to comment on body shapes and height. For some reason she especially disapproved of women in trousers. *"If I had a behind like that…!"* I had better stop there. Feeling you have the right to tell people exactly what you are thinking, even if it isn't polite may be a sign of aging but it was also due to Eunson genes.

On one of my visits to Orkney while on furlough from Peru, as I read a book, I was oblivious to her conversation to me. She gained my attention through a typical command: *"Kenneth get up! Come and stand over here! How tall are you?"* *"Five foot nine,"* I replied. *"That is a fine height,"* she responded approvingly. *"Your brother Robert is jist [7]*

---

[6] Orcadian for *"for goodness sake man speak right."*
[7] Orcadian for *"just."*

peedie[8] *and that is all you can say aboot*[9] *it."* Robert stands at five foot six inches! He would be considered a good height in Peru, but not from where mother sat. That is the important point.

My first introduction to a dead person was when we siblings were ushered in to see Grandfather Scott in a coffin in 1958. He looked much as he had in life, except dead. In 1959, when I was ten years of age, Granny Scott died of what Mother called a broken heart. Today, anorexia would have been mentioned as her way of grieving for her beloved husband. I was taken aback when I saw Granny in an emaciated state in the coffin. As we all sat there, Mother commented: *"Doesn't she look good in the coffin?"* Others agreed. In my thoughts I did not concur. She looked very dead! I have seen too many dead bodies since.

Words carry a meaning and the use of *"stupid"* has never carried a positive connotation for me. This became even more acute after living in Peru for over two decades. It is about as bad a human designation as any curse word in Spanish. When Mother asked me to hang up her washing on one of my visits to Orkney, she accompanied the request by adding: *"We will see whether you are stupid in how you do it!"* I understood, I think!

My sister Doreen accompanied me during another visit there. Imagine our initial shock when Mother offered her opinion that our father had been *"stupid."* I objected by challenging her: *"Mother you cannot say that."* *"I ken*[10], *but he was. He was always wrong, and I was right."* Doreen entered the conversation: *"But nobody is always wrong, and nobody is always right."* Mother went on: *"If I had been wrong, I would have admitted it, but he was always wrong, and I was right."* One more illustration of this will suffice. At a business meeting in the Baptist Church in Kirkwall, Father had just given his opinion on a matter when my mother voiced her evaluation of his: *"It is nothing of the kind!!!"*

Father had suffered yet another slight heart attack on one of my later visits from Northern Ireland and the doctor advised him to take to his bed. I wondered out loud to Mother whether he would appreciate having the television in the bedroom. *"No,"* Mother commented, *"why would he?"* I decided I should ask him. *"Oh, that would be grand,"* Father

---

[8] *"Peedie"* is an Orcadian word for small.
[9] Orcadian for *"about."*
[10] Meaning *"to know."*

19

smiled. I went in later, and he was contentedly lying on his side watching his afternoon TV programmes.

On return to the lounge Mother illuminated me into her distinctive way of thinking by explaining that she believed it was not wise to help old people too much before they simply needed it. Father was over nine years older than she was. It was, I surmised, a question of perspective from her relative youth and of how she viewed the world. The next day Father was puffing and panting as he attempted to pull on his socks in the morning. I still wonder if the help I gave him to get his socks on had staved off another heart attack. I think he needed help. To my knowledge Father pulled on his own socks until the day he died quietly in his chair in 1992.

On Saturday evening of the same week, Mother informed me that Father was asking for me. When I went to the bedroom, he presented me with a notebook and pen and asked me to go out to the garage to read and record the electricity meter. After accomplishing that mission Mother informed me with a smile that Father did so every Saturday evening just so he kept a control of electricity consumption and costs. After Father died in 1992, I later discovered that although Mother had dismissed his weekly pilgrimage to read the meter she had continued to do so until her death in 2010. Perhaps it represented her process of mourning. I suggest this because Jeannie and I also observed that all photos of Father were removed from albums and shelves.

Both parents had lived during World War II and the subsequent rationing. They certainly lived modestly. Waste was anathema. Evidence of frugality became more on view in retirement as teabags were rationed and recycled during the day. Mother claimed they could manage on one/day! She asserted that during her last eight years she had not bought any new clothes. She would declare, *"Why spend money on what you do not need?"* I always respected them for their thriftiness and should add that they gave generously to Christian Mission and to charities from their modest pensions.

I am amused when I remember Mother's dogmatism regarding the use of shortened or changed first names. *"If someone is given a name on their birth certificate then that form should be used,"* she would state. She seemed to forget that when she referred to my oldest brother Thomas as Tom, or to brother James Martin as just Martin, or to my father (John) as Johnnie, or to herself (Catherine) as Kitty. Everyone knew her as Kitty. Her ruling came into force as she always called Robert by his name, and not as Robbie, as he was affectionately known. I was always Kenneth and not Ken. Everyone knows me as Ken.

Orcadians were renowned for showing no public outward signs of affection. Any visitor from *"doon Sooth"*[11] was feared, especially if they insisted on giving someone a hug, or even worse, a kiss on the cheek. I never saw my parents exchange hugs or even one kiss. I was fully aware of that feature in my Orkney world. On Jeannie's first visit to Orkney in 1978 she was heavily pregnant with Samuel. It was Sunday afternoon, and we were sitting rather quietly at the table sharing lunch devoid of any conversation. I thought it time to liven things up, so with an exclamation gave Jeannie a big kiss on the cheek. Mother puckered up her lips with hands on her knees and, yes, Father sniggered quietly. I loved to make him smile.

The sibling-grapevine informed me within days that an authoritative evaluation of the event had been declared by Mother. *"It taks*[12] *Kenneth all his time."* I was happy with that as I knew my mother felt better placed to judge *"normality"* from her vantage point. I can vouch for the fact that my father could show affection to the dog. Years earlier I had overheard Mother mention that he showed more fondness for the dog than for her. His answer was profound: *"Weel!*[13]*"*

On a lighter note, I discovered that my mother had never eaten haggis in her lifetime. Cousin Irene and her husband Rev Jim Millar were present on that occasion. So it was that I decided to dictate the conditions. *"Mother you will have haggis for tea along with neeps*[14] *and tatties*[15] *provided you stay out of the kitchen."* *"Why?"* was her question. My reply: *"Just so you let me do it my way."* All went well until she decided she needed to water the plants in the kitchen! I was preparing some carrots *a la julienne* to mix with the swede to give them a sweeter taste. *"Mercy, what a stupid way to peel carrots. I hae*[16]*never seen anybody prepare carrots like that before in my life."* The story had a happy ending. She enjoyed her tea. Mother was a character for sure.

My brother Ivan recently sent me a photocopy of a two-page typescript entitled *"EUNSONS IN WESTRAY."* We believe that our Uncle Frank

---

[11] Down South.
[12] Meaning takes.
[13] Well!
[14] Turnips.
[15] Potatoes.
[16] Have.

Eunson wrote it, although we are open to the possibility that Uncle David Eunson (1932-2013), mother's second youngest brother, was the author. Be that as it may, I remember that I had read it well over a decade previously. On that occasion I mentioned to Mother that I would like a copy although I did not follow up on the request. After my return to Belfast Mother phoned to ask me to send it back as she could not find it, and I had been the last person to have seen it. I assured her that I did not take it. Did she believe me? Anyway, after she died, Ivan took ownership of the document from among Mother's possessions!

The author of the above-mentioned document, traces the presence of the Eunson lineage in Westray from somewhere before 1850 until they were no more on the island: *"With the death of Kitty Brown of Bonnie Doon in October 1991 there passed the last Westray inhabitant born a Eunson."* The final two sentences in the manuscript describe the Eunson distinctive that speaks for itself:

> *In other families a number of boys might have taken over the home croft or aspired to another farm. This was not the case with the Eunsons after 1900 so surely they were born to be servants not bosses, though anyone having heard a Eunson giving orders is not going to believe that!*

THE SCOTTS

Although I only went back as far as my grandfather on Mother's side of the family, my great grandfather John Scott on Father's side was also a Westray man. He was born in 1848 and after a short illness died at the age of 65 in 1914. What drew my attention to him was that besides being a landowner, he was renowned for his integrity, and he was *"responsible for the kelp-making industry on Col. Balfour's Trenabie Estate. By his firm yet tactful methods, and withal impartial justice, he won, in no slight degree, the esteem and confidence of the kelp-workers[17]."* One of his three sons was called Thomas Scott (1876-1958), Grandfather Scott.

What impressed me most regarding my great grandfather is his character and his connection to the Baptist Church on the Island of Westray. A series of quotations from the same document will highlight this:

---

[17] *Obituary written on the death of the late John Scott, of Gill Farm, Westray,* recorded in a local newspaper, on his funeral dated the 26th of February 1914.

Mr Scott was well-known and highly respected throughout the island, and by many outside of it.... He was sixty-five years of age, and by being thus cut of, as he was, in the midst of his activities, Mr Scott's removal will be much felt for many days to come.... Mr Scott had a life-long connection with the Baptist Church. He there for many years held the various offices of deacon, secretary, and treasurer ... for the long period of at least thirty-three years and perhaps longer.... He was a man with a simple yet real faith in the Lord. He read a good deal, and being endowed with a keen intellect, he held with a clear understanding and firm grasp those principles which are dear to us as a denomination.... Being a man of sterling character and worth, his testimony was always good, and his word, his bond. His wise words of counsel and cheer, as well as his kind acts, helped and encouraged many....

I discovered that most of the founding members of the Baptist Church in Kirkwall in 1959 can trace their ancestry back to my great grandfather's children, including my father, his grandson. I lament that when I came to rely on my own reminiscences of my father's parents, I have few memories. On a visit to Orkney in 2019 my older brother Robert's comments jolted me to recall Grandfather Scott as a very friendly person, while Grandmother Scott evoked in him a sterner recollection. I bow to that as accurate.

I carry three images of Grandfather Scott in my mind. The first one was quite simply of him speaking kindly to me when he came to our farm along with my father's brother Jim. When I close my eyes, I can still see his stocky figure, a couple of weeks before his death, trampling down the grass with his feet in the silage pit on his farm. I already mentioned the third occasion as he lay in his coffin. Sadly, I cannot remember anything of Granny Scott, except when I had been shocked by her emaciated form in her coffin.

Grandfather Thomas Scott (1876 -1958) married Ann Rendall (1882-1959), from Evie on the Mainland[18] of Orkney in December 1909 and they spent nearly five decades together. The same was true of Father, their oldest child, John Adams Scott (1911-1992) who married Catherine (Kitty) Eunson (1920-2010) in May 1942 in Westray. They spent almost fifty years together before also being separated by death. The Scotts were landowners and generations worked their way up in terms of land

---

[18] The largest island in Orkney is called Mainland.

ownership from smaller beginnings. When I arrived on the scene in 1949 my parents owned Howe Farm in the Parish of Harray, on Mainland. I was the fourth child, in a family that was to grow to a total of eight siblings.

In time Father acquired more property some seven miles away so that he owned approximately 330 acres of arable land. Beef cattle, sheep, laying hens and pigs required labour, and that extended to us boys. There were plenty ready-made chores to occupy us. We were expected to help, and I suspect my older three brothers probably started at a younger age than I did. Affirmation was not Father's style, nor did the week stop at lunchtime on Saturdays.

Father had never been shy of work and one of his enduring qualities was that he did not ask others to do what he would not do himself. He never used bad language, and, like Mother, he had little time for braggarts. Another feature that I respected was his biblical understanding that church and state should be separate. The Church of Scotland was the state church and landowners were required by law to pay an annual stipend. He objected in principle but always paid his taxes. This integrity was part of who he was.

Work increased at the weekends in Winter as the farm workers signed off on Saturdays at lunchtime. Animals still had to be fed, and on Sundays of all days. Our duties were good preparation for later life and as I grew up, I increasingly enjoyed working alongside Father, older brothers, and the men employed on the farm. Physical activity always felt good.

I spent two years working on the family farm (1966-1968) after leaving Stromness Academy before I went to England to study for Christian ministry and then another short stint living at home (1971-1973) when I worked as a pastor in Orkney. I treasure fond memories of occasions that Father and I discussed our common faith in Christ as we worked together. There followed a gap of five years (1973-1978) in Peru and away from Orkney. It was while studying Spanish in Costa Rica (1973-1974) that I met Jeannie and later married her on the 28th of December in 1974.

On our first furlough from Peru with Jeannie, our daughter Rebecca and soon-to-be-born Samuel I discovered Father had mellowed in character after retirement. By then they lived in a bungalow in Kirkwall, Orkney's capital. Both parents continued to be non-extravagant, thrifty, and modest in their lifestyles. I remember well that Father dug his extensive vegetable garden eighteen inches deep. He worked slowly and rested regularly. By then he had already suffered a heart attack.

To save expense he would buy an entire sheep and would carve up the carcass himself. He accepted my offer of help which involved hoisting the entire cadaver to the low beams in the garage. His methodology involved sawing from the tail to the neck by using a dull crosscut saw designed for woodwork. At his insistence he began the task but stopped to catch his breath after managing to advance very little. It was time for me to take over and not let him back in. It was hard work, but it was worth it as I might have staved off another incident with his heart.

I like cabbage, but because Father majored on growing that vegetable Mother felt obliged to grace the lunch table with it. I remember asking brother George if he liked Father's greens. He replied: *"No every day!"* The neighbours were given plentiful supplies as Father used to throw them over the wall without wasting energy by telling them. He expected them to collect their own supply of blessings that flew in. That was fine until one household went on holiday for two weeks without telling Father!!! Their supply of cabbages continued in their absence.

All I have told is the truth but not the whole truth. Both parents were unique and veritable characters. I will always be thankful for their legacies of integrity, straight talking, thriftiness, hard work and faith in God. Their beliefs became mine and during my life I have sought to share the message of Jesus with others.

FINAL REFLEXIONS

As a boy, I enjoyed the excitement of Santa Claus, my predictable Mars bar, Caramac Caramel Bar, orange, and apple in my stocking, and the accompanying gift. Even when my older brother Ivan clarified the truth about Christmas, when I became a little man of six, it remained special!!! My mother's annoyance with me when I told her that I knew who Santa Claus was met with a rebuff: *"Who has been filling your head with that nonsense?"* I am sure she was simply wanting to recreate the joy she felt from her memories of Christmas in her own rather poorer background.

I contend that formation starts early, and I will always be thankful that mine began with God. There was never a confusion in my mind between the mythology of Santa Claus and the truth regarding Jesus. The message communicated to my heart as a boy was that Jesus Christ was God's only Son who humbled himself enough to be human. This meekness led Jesus to die on the cross so that we could be right with God. It amazed me that God in human flesh showed no smugness, no aloofness, no entitlement, and no disdain for humanity. On the contrary Jesus showed love and called people to follow him.

If Jesus could do that for me and make me a child of the living God, I understood that to be the purest demonstration of grace possible. As God's child I was called to hold nothing back from God and, like Jesus, to hold nothing back from others who equally needed the same grace. The issue that followed for me has always been to decipher how to understand what that means in practice.

PRAYER

Heavenly Father, I know you love me, accept me, and cherish me. Thank you for adopting me as your child and for loving me unconditionally. I know I fall short of your glory every day. Help me by your grace to strive to be more like you. Amen

Not long before Mother died, I recall a memorable conversation I had with her. I had been sharing that Jeannie and I regretted that we had ever used physical punishment on our children. To be honest, in my case, it only happened once with each of our two children. In response she changed tack and related her apprehension of when Father had expressed regrets in life and struggled to articulate his faith in God shortly before he died. Mother's take on the matter was clear: *"Surely Kenneth you will have no regrets when you come to die."*

I believe, as did Mother, that God wipes the slate clean when we come to him in true repentance; nevertheless, I do have regrets. Another memory comes to mind to reinforce my thinking. When I was fifteen years of age, I attended a Christian Endeavour camp near Alloa in Scotland. Afterwards I heard Pastor Derek Prime preach in Charlotte Chapel Baptist Church in Edinburgh. I still envisage his dapper appearance in a pinstripe suit as he said, *"the closer we draw to God the darker the shadow of personal sin will seem. Just as when we place our hands near to a light the bigger the shadow will become."*

I will always consider the late Jim Stockan, an Orkney businessperson who focussed on producing good oatcakes, which continue to carry his surname, to have had a major influence on my life. After studying in England (1968-1971) I pastored Dounby United Free Church of Scotland in Orkney (1971-1973). Jim and his lovely wife May gave me of their time and shared tray bakes and cups of tea with me. Those times usually ended in prayer.

For the sake of brevity here, I remember Jim's counsel that in my desire to follow the Lord I would make missteps. He told me he had known Christian leaders who admitted to no mistakes to the point of believing themselves to be infallible. Jim had a way of repeating things! For instance, I learned, and cannot forget, that *"the glory must always be for the Lord because the Lord does not share His glory."* I also recall him reiterating: *"Ken, if you are ever accused and are guilty, hands up to the Lord. If you are not guilty as accused, hands up to the Lord!"* I have never neglected that and have had to practise both approaches on occasions!

From those discussions I factored into my life the ideas of not needing to defend myself and of not dropping someone else into the frame. Biblical texts illustrate that the Lord does not share his glory. One such example is: *"I am the Lord; that is my name! I will not give my glory to anyone else, nor share my praise with carved idols"* (Isaiah: 42:8). In the same way there are passages that illustrate God's willingness to move me on from mistakes and to make up for lost time. *"The Lord says, 'I will give you back what you lost to the swarming locusts.... Then, after doing all those things, I will pour out my spirit upon all people'"* (Joel 2:25, 28).

WHO COMES SECOND?

In my zeal to serve the Lord as a missionary, to evangelize, and extend the Lord's work I was often away from home for weeks at a time. For the sake of brevity here I can relate that this was so when Jeannie and I lived in Peru during our first term of service as a married couple (1975-1991). When our daughter Rebecca was still quite small, I had travelled to remote villages during our time in Chalhuanca, Apurímac (1975-1978). On return from one extended trip, it was painful to realize that Rebecca did not recognize me!

Years later (1983) I returned home to Abancay, Apurímac, with a Peruvian co-worker called Jacob, for just three days, from a long tour to the Province of Grau. I recall Jeannie's frustrated reaction when I informed her that, as Field Co-ordinator, I was due to travel again, this time to Amazonas in the North of Peru. She replied: *"Just go!"*

During the following two weeks I had time to reflect. I calculated that I sat on a bus for eight days altogether. The good news about that trip was that I travelled, along with a leader of the Peruvian Evangelical Church (Saúl Barrera) so that seventeen churches, planted by RBMU missionaries Fred and Ruth Webb, May Walker, Elaine Webster and David and Helena Stevens, could join the Peruvian denomination. I was doing the Lord's work and thus justified my absence yet again!

It was not just a matter of physical absence, but of ordering priorities in life. Later, when working as Director of Studies in the Belfast Bible College (1991-1999), long weekdays and Saturdays were spent in my office in preparing lectures and looking after students' needs, planning timetables, lecturer's schedules, and record keeping, while preaching every weekend, completely consumed my life. Rebecca, by then sixteen years of age, did a work-placement at the College while pursuing her grammar school studies at the Methodist College, Belfast. She will never know how deeply her question stabbed at my heart and conscience: *"Dad, do you love the students at college more than me?"*

When Jeannie and I left Belfast again (2000-2007) to collaborate with Baptist Missions in South Peru, our children, Rebecca and Samuel, now young adults, stayed on in our house in Belfast. A similar pattern emerged. Total commitment to the task in hand. A Seminary to set up in Tacna, a Radio Station to begin, a new role of Project Manager in state-of-the-art construction projects, networking in Lima, and administrative matters to address. It was in August of 2005 that Samuel's cancer diagnosis led Jeannie to return home ahead of me for four months to help him through.

Something had to break in me. There was a log in the way of me establishing biblical priorities. I had it wrong. It was not a sequence of God first, ministry second, and then family. There was no doubt in my heart that the Lord was to be first but what came next? My confusion related to the place of family in relation to God. Christian ministry had driven me on as of prime importance.

All that began to shift when I started to acknowledge my family as my first responsibility after the Lord. As I write this, I cannot thank God enough that Jeannie and I now live near to our children and grandchildren in Northern Ireland. This is the best time of my life and a point in time to deal with that log. Is it ever too late for the Lord to restore the *"years the locusts have eaten?"*

MISPLACED ZEAL

When still a young man a knock-on effect of my desire to follow the Lord led to aggressive evangelism. This was so on a personal level, in outreach on the streets and in pubs and clubs. A select number from a list of examples will suffice. I well-remember preaching on the streets of Birmingham one night in 1970 when two young police officers told me to move on. I am ashamed of my reply: *"I come to you in the authority of the King of Kings! In whose authority do you come to me?"* They politely shrugged their shoulders and left me to it. Who knows what they thought? That was ignorant on my part and gracious of them.

This approach to preaching the Gospel came home to me as inappropriate when soon after arriving in Northern Ireland in 1991, my son Samuel and I had ventured into Belfast. Life was still fraught with unpredictability due to the *"Troubles."* An elderly gentleman, accompanied with placards and biblical texts, was preaching on the street as we passed: *"You are going to hell the lot of you!"* Samuel replied: *"Well, I am not!"*

I suppose that I had imbibed a certain evangelical mindset that encouraged a limited social life. To avoid following the ways of the *"world"* specified activities were off limits. The list of questionable behaviour could vary from church to church, but included events such as dances, dress, the use of alcohol, certain sports, and the cinema. For a Christian to attend such places or to be part of designated *"worldly"* activities was unwholesome. To be fair, we had little time to be involved because of chores and church meetings as we grew up.

During the two years (1966-1968) that I worked on the home farm before going to Bible College in England I called my older brother Ivan to task for taking Moira, his girlfriend and later his wife, to the cinema. Mother had previously voiced her concern about going there. It did not occur to me at that time that the Sound of Music film might just be wholesome entertainment. I have since moved on in my thinking although discretionary viewing of certain material is necessary.

LIFE'S MISTAKES

The fact that the Bible teaches that God knows the worst about us and yet persists with us has been a comfort in life. The corollary to that is the hiddenness of God from worshippers who are insincere. There is no doubt that the presence of unconfessed sin not only alienates a believer from God but that it saddles a person with guilt. I suppose that I would articulate these as the ways of God and the paths of life and death.

It would achieve little to make a list of a litany of my sins and hence of a similar register of regrets. Other *"logs"* that have needed to be dealt with appear in future chapters. Jesus clarified that doing something incorrect was on a par to thinking a wrong thought. In that regard, an inconsiderate word would be the same as a curse, insincerity a lie, hatred the very act of murder, meanness equal to theft, and lust equivalent to committing adultery.

It is one thing to testify to eternal life by knowing God and Jesus Christ sent by him (John 17:3) but it is something else to forget the question of ultimate divine judgement. To ignore God's justice is to make repentance virtually unthinkable. Three verses from Scripture written to Christians have continually reminded me of the need for ongoing repentance and faith in God. They are in 1 John 1:8-10:

> *[8] If we claim we have no sin, we are only fooling ourselves and not living in the truth. [9] But if we confess our sins to him,*

he is faithful and just to forgive us our sins and to cleanse us from all wickedness. [10] If we claim we have not sinned, we are calling God a liar and showing that his word has no place in our hearts.

Having rejected the idea of making a list of sins committed by me over the years, I wish to turn my attention to a persistent failing that calls me back to the Lord in repentance repeatedly. I cannot remember my father or mother, or my siblings, for that matter, ever using bad language. There has never been any doubt in my mind that our speech should be free from what we called swearing. Above all, liberty is from the light use of the name of God, from expletives, and the needless invocation of God's name in common speech. That can only lead in the end to irreverence. That has not ever been something I have had to struggle with as it was inbred into me.

While using bad language is not a personal struggle, the avoidance of even a hint of gossip is another story. The one is as bad as the other. God cleans up a person's mouth when that individual trusts in him and seeks to follow him. Faith in Jesus Christ enables us to be wholeheartedly right with each other and with God. We practise a devotion to the truth with our lips because the truth lives in us in the person of the Holy Spirit. I have witnessed this in the lives of true believers on many occasions.

Believers are all made God's children through the Word of truth! A controlled tongue is the evidence of God's blessing and the key to holy living. Is it not James, the Lord's half-brother who writes that if we control the tongue, we control the whole body (James 3:2)? The management of one's speech is more than evidence of spiritual maturity it is the means to it. In a world where many are hostile to the very idea of God, my use of language makes its presence felt, either leaving a stain and making me offensive to God or pleasing to him.

The new nature in Christ does not solve the conflict in our everyday speech, nor do we have an automatic victory in life in what we may say. We are born for battle and the old nature, and the new nature fight it out. Growth into the image of Jesus is a prolonged struggle, an effort against the odds. The combat winds uphill all the way to the very end. While there is always proof of the Lord's work of grace in our hearts, growth in sanctification is our direct responsibility and at its core are the words we employ. This is especially so regarding people. I pray that I reach a place where I never use denigrating words in this respect. Hasten the day that I do the Lord's bidding in this consistently.

It is my experience that other vices drop off with age, but the misuse of the tongue continues. The employment of harmful words is certainly evidence of the Devil's activity. I wish to draw this to a close and declare the matter for what it is. In Matthew 12:34 we read, *"For whatever is in your heart determines what you say."* I suspect I am not alone in this ongoing battle. Expressed simply: defamatory, unloving speech issues from a heart where the love of Jesus is not present.

THE INNER PHARISEE

I wish to allude to the one non-Jewish writer of Scripture, Dr Luke, to illustrate my next point. In chapter seven of his Gospel, Luke recounts an encounter Jesus had with a Roman Centurion (7:1-10) who sent Jewish religious leaders to Jesus to plead on his behalf that the Lord would go to his house to heal one of his much-loved servants. Before Jesus arrived at his house the God-fearing Roman again sent messengers for Jesus to *"say the word only"* for healing. The narrative clarifies that the Roman soldier does not feel he deserves Jesus to be near him nor even enter his house. Jesus was amazed at the man's humility and trust and declared that he had not witnessed anything akin to this faith in all Israel.

In the same chapter of his gospel, Luke writes another moving story (Luke 7:36-50) of how an unnamed woman, perhaps a prostitute, arrived in the home of a Pharisee named Simon, where Jesus had been invited for a meal. Simon and those present experienced negative thoughts when the woman bowed at Jesus feet and wiped his tear-covered feet with her hair, kissed his feet and finally poured expensive perfume over them.

In response to the disdain present in Simon's heart, Jesus told a parable of two men who were forgiven their debts to a moneylender. One man owed a modest amount while the other owed an exorbitant amount: both were forgiven. Jesus' question to Simon was about which of the two loved the financier more. In reply, Simon supposed that the one who had been forgiven the greater debt loved the lender more.

Jesus, who knows everyone's heart, turns to the woman, and declares that her sins are forgiven. Further judgemental thoughts are directed towards Jesus for not discerning *"the kind of woman"* he is dealing with. The condescension is envisaged as evidence that Jesus is not who he claims to be. Jesus is surely teaching that whoever is forgiven much loves Jesus much and whoever is forgiven little loves Jesus little.

I identify with the first story and with the fact that the Centurion, who had heard from others about Jesus, chose to trust him. I relate also to the woman in the second story whose *"many"* sins are forgiven. Nevertheless, it is with Simon, the pharisee, that I connect. It has been too easy to disassociate myself from the lady in the story and, like Simon, to hold someone in disdain because I have not transgressed like that person. When I do so, I am equally guilty of the pernicious evil of self-righteousness, just as Simon is in the story. It has taken me a lifetime to realize that as a professing Christian I have been guilty of seeing the hypocritical pharisee in someone else, but seldom in me.

Since retirement in 2014, part of my daily routine is to walk at least five miles every day. In that context I meet new people and am learning that the Lord has a bigger family than I imagined, right on my doorstep. I chat to unchurched people and learn of their daily realities and am continually surprised to discover true faith in the Lord among them. As to fellow Christians, denominational preferences, lifestyle, style of worship and liturgy, are but a few of the factors that predicate inner judgement.

As I step back from public ministry I am drawn into a journey of discovery. Another world is open to me. I had gone to Peru as a missionary, had even lived in the vicinity in Belfast for several years, but did not know what God is doing in the lives of my neighbours. My role is not to emit value judgements from a place of safety but to learn from others that the Lord was here long before I came on the scene. Pride is the worst sin of all, and I have been forgiven much. May I love Jesus and others accordingly.

I am always surprised when Christians object to the idea of our sin and sins, as if somehow Christ's work has already made us perfect. I find myself identifying with King David who had no such illusion about his own heart when he wrote (Psalm 19: 12-14):

> *[12] How can I know all the sins lurking in my heart? Cleanse me from these hidden faults. [13] Keep your servant from deliberate sins! Do not let them control me. Then I will be free of guilt and innocent of great sin. [14] May the words of my mouth and the meditation of my heart be pleasing to you, O Lord, my rock, and my redeemer.*

I am more aware of my innate sinfulness now than at any time in my life and of how glorious Jesus is in the forgiveness offered to me and to all who trust in God. Jesus is at the centre of both encounters in Luke's account and is he not comparing himself to the moneylender who freely forgives his debtors?

Is it not so that each time we who follow Christ *"eat"* bread and *"drink"* wine at the Lord's Table we thank the Lord again for his atoning death on the cross and remember that event as the most important fact for all humanity? At the same time, I am exercised about the need to root out the inner pharisee, all-too present at times, and of practising the U-turn required through true repentance.

PRAYER

Our Father and our God, your radiance blinds us. We cannot look on the brilliance of your purity and holiness without repenting of our sinfulness, and of the ugly stains on our hearts and souls. We pray for your forgiveness to wash our souls clean again, as white as snow. Lord, we cannot live without you. In Jesus' name we pray. Amen

Jeannie post university studies but pre-Ken

Spanish studies in Costa Rica pre-Jeannie – 1973

Fellow students in San José Costa Rica in late 1973. Jeannie is in the centre and Ken in blue shirt

Our first date out for a meal in San José, Costa Rica – December 1973. Check out the dress code!

In the United States in February 1974 and happily on the way to buy a ring!

Bethany Beach, Delaware on our engagement

Engaged on the 22nd of February 1974

Our wedding in Greenwood Mennonite Church on the 28th of December 1974

Abancay, Apurimac - 1975. Stewart and late wife Janet and their children – Alison, Ruth, Rachel, and John. Far right: Chris, and late wife Jacqui Papworth with Cherry Noble. Jeannie (and Rebecca!) and me in the centre, accompanied by short termers

Abancay again in 1983

In Lima in 1985

Father and Mother in later life
pre 1986

In Lima just before travelling to
work in the Belfast Bible College
in 1991

Back in Peru with Baptist Missions – the completed Seminary
auditorium in Tacna in 2004

Ken teaching in the Baptist Seminary in 2004

The completed Sower Radio building in Tacna in 2006

Administration in the Sower Radio soon before leaving Tacna for ministry in the Irish Baptist College – 2007

Modern Lima, skyscrapers and old colonial buildings

Modern Lima, the sprawl of cities

Mother's 90th birthday celebrations after the event on the 4th of April 2010. Back: Martin, Alistair, George, and me. Front: Ivan, Tom, Mother, Doreen, and Robert

Jeannie and Rebecca at Sam and Deb's wedding

Samuel David Scott just married to Deborah Mary Edith Quinn on 29th of May 2021

Ganesh and Rebecca with Anjali and Ajay

Ajay with me on Sam and Deb's wedding day

Celebrating my 72nd birthday with Ajay and Anjali – 30th of January 2021

CHAPTER 3   ANGER

It would be easier not to write this chapter and to skim over this personal human weakness. Nevertheless, it is my desire to put into words what I know to be true, while remaining cognizant of the fact that what I explain will still be a potted account. My purpose is to highlight another log that is still in danger of remaining and thus blurring my vision.

When I committed my life to Christ as a boy, I knew that I needed to deal with my temper. I was not angry all the time but when I felt cornered or bullied it was instinctive for me to lash out and fight. As much as I loved my father, I perceived his anger as a constant that led to discipline and to constant rebukes, even when I did not understand what I might have done. I knew that he did not know another way and I learned to read him for signs of approval. My anger, on the other hand, was sporadic and was an inward response to bullying and to other people's annoyance.

Nevertheless, I do testify to a change in outlook as I sought by prayer to avoid playground fights. That was my world. Indeed, I even knew biblical counsel on the subject: *"Avoiding a fight is a mark of honour; only fools insist on quarrelling"* (Proverbs 20:3). I understood faith in the Lord to be the common mark of all Christians, and in my thinking, I exercised mine by asking Jesus to help me be principled enough to avoid scrapping.

I wish I could relate that as the end to it. On entering Stromness Academy in 1961 I encountered bullies. As I communicate elsewhere in the book, I was the smallest in the family at that age along with my sister Doreen. Mother's red book records that we were both only four foot seven and a half inches tall on our respective twelfth birthdays. So it was that the tough guys came after me in their twos or threes.

There were several skirmishes in which I always came off the worse against greater numbers. The inevitable happened when at thirteen years of age, while my body clock had still annoyingly refused to let me grow bigger, that I turned on two bullies. It was a classic school fight! This time only one member of the gang fought me, while the other, and half the school, or so it seemed to me, created a ring around us and cheered us on. I had to win as I was tired of looking over my shoulder most days. To be sure, I was left alone after that and enjoyed my new-found status. Nevertheless, I felt ashamed that I had let the Lord down.

By the time I reached the age of seventeen, I had grown to my full stature of five foot nine inches, and my gangly bones were covered with just enough for me to weigh in at 147 pounds. I was not the one being intimidated, but I did not hesitate when I saw a six-foot two-inch classmate – we will call him *"Shoes"* – bully a much smaller pupil, who had been in two classes below me in Primary School. I remember flooring *"Shoes."*

That was not the end to it. On the way up the hill to Brinkie's Brae to join classmates for a game of football, I was oblivious at first as to what caused the excruciating pain in both kidneys. *Shoes* had taken me out from behind with two well-placed punches. It took for what seemed like an eternity for the pain to pass and for me to be able to get up and continue up to the playing field. I remember being relieved and thinking that was it all sorted, tit for tat. That feeling was to be short-lived!

On arrival for the match, I overheard *Shoes* boasting to classmates that he had given me a *"good hiding."* The *"log"* was immediately there in my eye and the button had been pressed. *"You great liar"* was what I shouted as I went in with both fists. I did not stop until *Shoes* went down. The end to that combat came in our next woodwork class. *Shoes* kept on deliberately jostling me every time the teacher's back was turned. By then my anger had subsided, and remorse had set in. I looked *Shoes* out. *"Hey Shoes, I am sorry for my behaviour."* He replied: *"No hard feelings."* That was that.

Father was a man of law and order and was known for his integrity. Whenever he saw policemen, he would lower his voice and encouraged us to do the same. I did wonder if he had ever had a brush with the Police. Whatever was the case, he had warned me about the fate of my Cairn Terrier, Peter (named after Peter Scott the famous conservationist, television presenter, and much more), if he was turned into the Police Station in Kirkwall again for following his hormones to other farms. This happened for the second, or maybe the third time, on Father and Mother's Silver Wedding Anniversary in May 1967.

I loved my dog Peter and had already taken him to the Vet on an occasion when a nameless farmer had successfully made two holes in his abdomen with a pitchfork. On that auspicious day Mother had been slaving over preparing a roast turkey meal and dessert. Now, there is a story! Before everything was ready Father informed me that I should bury my dog. I saw red, and as far as I can remember never spoke back to my father, either before that fateful day, or afterwards as I did then.

"You killed my dog, you bury him" was my reply. I never knew, and did not want to know, where my three-year-old terrier was buried but was livid because of what had happened. I knew I had to forgive Father.

I vaguely remember eating a full meal that evening and then, in a mode to show off, ate twelve raw eggs. Strange as this may appear to a reader, I was so angry I could have eaten twenty-four eggs. It took me days to pardon Father, and to ask forgiveness from the Lord. I digress as I remember occasions when invited out for a meal by so-called Christians who were rude, for example, either about the food, or about the table service. My form of protest was always to refuse to ask for more than either the smallest item on the menu or just a coffee. Other people's rudeness or anger takes my appetite from me, and invariably elicits a silent protest.

I admit that over the years anger springs up in me on occasions. On the other hand, an angry, rude person, is enough to make me boil. For the most part the Lord enabled me to be self-controlled and not to react. In my final year of studies in the now non-existent Birmingham Bible Institute (1968-1971), my girlfriend sent me a letter to let me know she had found someone else. She and her husband-to-be were fine folk, and I was relieved. I always knew I would never marry her because my heart was set on working in Peru while she was not. I was at peace.

Father saw it differently, and I did not understand why he took it upon himself to comment on the matter when I returned to Orkney from my studies. Mother and my sister Doreen were present when Father commented that I had *"made a fool"* of myself because of the broken relationship. His comments were unwelcomed. Further, I did not break the courtship! I was grateful to the Lord for the grace to simply leave the room as the most appropriate non-verbal response. Anyway, I had already vowed to the Lord that the next girl I went out with would be my wife. More than two years had to pass before I met Jeannie!

Father had many redeeming qualities, one of which was to acknowledge that people who professed faith in Jesus from other Christian confessions were part of true Christianity. I remember his comments regarding a Seventh Day Adventist (SDA) salesman he met in Orkney and a *"genuine"* Roman Catholic believer with whom he transacted a business deal. In my later travels in Peru, a Catholic country, where the SDA Church flourished alongside the many evangelical churches, I came to the same conclusion regarding *"genuine"* believers in Jesus. I regularly met an Adventist for fellowship in Tacna, Peru (2000-2007)

46

and met several equally *"genuine"* Roman Catholic believers over decades in Peru. Lack of respect for sincerely held different Christian views has never seemed right to me. I recorded one such pre-Peru experience that did not meet with my approval when I wrote [19]:

> *It was in July of 1971 that I also visited Northern Ireland for the first time. There was much unrest at that time, and I witnessed the military presence in Belfast. Besides preaching on the streets, I took part in a march on July the 12th! I was invited to hear Dr Ian Paisley preach in his church on Sunday. I admit I was in awe of his physical presence and style as he entered the pulpit and observed the congregation. In fact, I remember his text and its delivery – "The flesh profiteth nothing" but could not for the life of me understand how in his sermon he interpreted this to mean "the outward trappings of the Catholic Church." Nor did I appreciate how he developed his theme from the text to make the assertion that "they (the Catholics) believe you receive grace through your stomach." I understood this to be a reference to the Mass but have never been convinced that the pulpit should be used to attack something that is sacred to so many.*

In late 1973 Walt, a young American joined me in the adjacent room, in the house where I had acquired full board in a Costa Rican home. His parents were paying for him to study Spanish with a view to his being able to pursue a bilingual line of work. Walt was aware from the beginning that I was also studying in the *Instituto de Lengua Española* with the purpose of working in Peru as a Christian missionary.

He seemed to take pleasure after our first meeting of taunting me by using profane language and by employing various forms of God's name as an adjective. I remember politely asking Walt to refrain from his misuse of the Lord's name. That only made it worse. I had imbibed my father's disdain for what he termed blasphemous language, and, I suppose, I shared that view then, and still do. So it was that one afternoon after a morning of Spanish studies Walt seemed bent on excelling in his abuse. I simply wanted to study the Spanish I had learned in class that morning whereas he was going out of his way to be the brat that I considered him to be.

---

[19] Ken Scott, *Life Stories of an Unworthy Servant,* lulu.com, January 2020, 11.

What happened next was not premeditated. As Walt continued to be more prolific in his colourful language, he walked past the sofa where I was seated. My spontaneous reaction was to grab him by the buckle on his belt and with another action, undoubtedly impelled by adrenalin, pinned him down. During his fruitless struggles, I remember uttering my ultimatum. *"Walt if you ever use the Lord's name like that again in my presence, I will flatten you."* After one more attempt to free himself from my grip I raised my right fist.

Walt never swore again within my hearing. I admit that I am not proud of what I did, although I still know that I would have carried out my threat. That was then. Walt became a committed Christian about two weeks later and cleaned up his act. He confessed afterwards that he was testing my reaction although he had not anticipated my aggression. When I travelled back from Peru to the United States to marry Jeannie on the 28th of December in 1974, we were delighted that Walt had agreed to be our official wedding photographer.

I admit that I have always been shocked by the disdain with which Christians can regard others who carry another *"label."* My introduction to Peru illustrates this[20]:

> *On arrival in Jorge Chávez Airport in Lima on the 20th of April 1974, a lady in an elegant dress and immaculate hairdo, with a US southern drawl, asked me if I was Ken Scott. After acknowledging the fact, I asked how she had guessed, to which she replied: "You look British!" I never knew what that meant especially as the plaid jacket I wore was bought in the USA and given to me by Jeannie. Ah, those were different times! I suppose that with hair covering my ears, a moustache, flared hipster trousers and a fitted jacket with lapels as broad as my shoulders I stood out from any American young man. I noticed thereafter that many American men at that time wore their trousers a couple of inches above their shoes.*
>
> *The lady was Dotty Battle and she announced that we needed to wait for Malone. I asked who Malone was and she replied that she called him Malone, whereas others knew him as Cooper Battle. They were American missionaries in Regions Beyond Missionary Union and Cooper was the man in Lima who took care of administration. My first impression of Malone/Cooper*

---

[20] Ibid, 17-20.

was of a not-so-immaculate husband, whose trousers were hanging down over a protruding tummy, jacket hanging off his shoulders, with glasses poised on the point of his nose and who was talking to himself. His trousers scuffed the ground! Without any introduction he gave the order: "Scott get in!" Silence ensued as I sat in the back seat of his double cabin pickup. He spoke in English (I think) only to Dotty as we travelled, and I cannot remember if I understood anything. On arrival at their home, I was invited to sit down. Cooper then announced: "I do not like Pentecostals". I remember stating that I was not Pentecostal. I feel I have had to clarify this many times since to many different people. Ah well, anyway, I came to quite like Cooper, in time.

The next day I was given instructions by Cooper to get on a certain bus and to get off at "migraciones" (immigration offices) and to present my documents along with other papers given to me by him. I did ask for some more clarification about landmarks, and, to this day, I do not know how I managed. I also remember instructions that on return I should help in Cooper's print shop. I got on well with the young Peruvian who worked for him. Unfortunately, I cannot remember his name. After a lapse of a few days, I was sent on the bus daily to enquire after progress on the visa and then to work in the print shop. I confess that, besides being attentive on each trip, I asked the Lord to help me not get lost. I remember that I was having a lot of stomach trouble on arrival from Costa Rica with all the ensuing delicate risks! This continued for some years in Peru. More of that later. Nevertheless, I was finally to be given my non-immigrant resident visa on the 14th of May....

I will never forget my first RBMU Field Conference at the end of November 1974 in a Southern Baptist Mission Centre in Chaclacayo, outside Lima. By the end of 1974 I had begun to realize that the American and the UK missionary contingents had had different opinions for some time regarding the relationship between the Mission and Peruvian denominations, and regarding the understanding and acceptability of Pentecostal doctrine and practice. The penny finally dropped with me when I met two RBMU North American missionaries for the first time. At Conference we three had just washed our hands in the bathroom when, without a handshake being offered, or introductions being made, I was challenged about my beliefs regarding the Holy Spirit. I was asked directly whether I had ever lost control and been thrown to the floor at any time. I believe that I replied graciously (on the outside), without even trying to explain my beliefs, that when God deigned to bless me, as in any case, I had never been more in control of my faculties. Déjà vu.

Jeannie and I spent over eight very happy years in Northern Ireland (1991-2000) where I worked as Director of Studies, and lecturer, and Jeannie headed up the Women's Study Fellowship in the Belfast Bible College. We returned to Tacna, Peru with Baptist Missions in early 2000. Very soon after arriving in South Peru, I was surprised by a pickpocket coming from behind and thrusting his hand in my trouser pocket where I carried money and my Peruvian identity documents.

Jeannie was equally surprised and wondered why he had come from behind to greet me! Reactions are instantaneous, although thoughts race at a moment like that. Everything stopped and Peruvians cheered: *"Ay gringo!"* Against common sense and tested wisdom, I lined him up for a right fist across his face, when he chose to grab the Peruvian currency that had fallen to the ground while at the same, throwing my documents and credit cards to the sidewalk. It was only then that I released him and opted for the documents. The hassle of replacing them loomed large in my thinking and the £15 worth of stolen cash was a small price to pay.

A couple of weeks later, with that fresh in my mind, Jeannie and I were walking to the *Koyuki* Restaurant for our Sunday lunch, when another young man attempted the same. This time I was ready because I only had a set of keys in my pocket, which he dropped immediately in disgust. By that time, much to my non-violent Mennonite wife's surprise, I had winded my attacker by kicking him in the stomach. Jeannie was amazed I could kick so high. We both lined up for a fight when I think he wisely decided to run away. A kind taxi driver stopped and offered me his advice: *"Gringo, don't be so rough on the guy, he probably needed the money!"*

Not long after that, Jeannie and I were just about to turn into the path to the Post Office to collect our mail, when I heard someone running up behind us. I was ready that time! I swung around and was about to hit the man as he veered past me to get on the bus that had stopped for him! I am including these stories as tangible evidence, as in the latter case, of what has led us to recall the events with laughter.

During our stint in Peru with Baptist Missions it was a joy to help set up the *Seminario Evangélico Bautista del Sur del Perú* in Tacna. That led me into the task like that of a Project Director in the construction of state-of-the-art buildings. I had already employed builders to construct a new three storey building and to carry out extensive repairs after an earthquake struck in 2001. It was in 2003 that work began on an auditorium and I had endeavoured to make sure that all materials were bought and ready, as well as following the plans meticulously. My take on that is that the building foreman had sought to cut corners every time I was not there. It happened once too often for me when I detected a flow of water through an already-constructed wall.

I had previously warned the foreman, that if he had to retrace his steps again to keep to the plans, I would sack him. Firstly, he denied there was a leak, and secondly, he indicated that I could not fire him and, thirdly, when he realized I was serious, that I should pay him over the odds. I saw red! Before I realized it, I had grabbed him and was about to land a punch. I caught myself on, and when Jeannie saw me enter our flat, she asked: *"Are you O.K.?" "No!"* I replied: *"I almost hit a man."*

Jeannie and I served with Baptist Missions in Peru from early 2000 until September 2007. After returning to Northern Ireland, I took up a part-time post in the Irish Baptist College as Postgraduate Director from January 2008 until retirement in January 2014. Jeannie was employed in the Faith Mission bookshop in Lisburn during that same time. For my part I returned to Peru twenty times between 2008 and 2019. It was during my fifteenth visit (7th June – 18th July) in 2017 that I was robbed at gunpoint on the 25th of June.

I had returned from church to the Baptist Mission flat on the third floor, in the 3 *de diciembre* district of Tacna, when my doorbell rang several times. To my surprise, as I looked over the balcony, I was greeted by an apparently overjoyed man: *"Hello Pastor, how great to find you in at last."* I asked: *"Do you know me?"* He shouted back that he had asked in the flat below and had been directed to me.

When I went down and met my visitor, he asked if he might come in, and then began to weep and pour out his woes and expressed his need for counsel. Something was not quite right, so I made the decision to cross the street to a Seminary classroom in the 5 *de noviembre* district of the city. I reasoned that the Peruvian employees of the Mission would soon be back from church. They never came.

It was when I entered the classroom and sat down at one of the desks that my visitor sat down opposite me with his back to the glass doors and pulled his gun and declared that he had another one in a back pocket. He proceeded to explain that he was connected to the Mafia – I think not - and showed me his battle scars on his upper torso. I knew I was in a sticky spot when he proceeded to mention that he only needed a thousand American dollars! I had the equivalent of 200 dollars in Peruvian currency in my pocket but did not want to part with it. I was angry.

Such occasions lead to inward prayer, and I was wondering who would tell Jeannie if something went wrong. I was sorely tempted to believe that my opportunity had come when he laid his gun on his desk, kneeled before me, and begged me for the money. I thought – *this is my moment, I could take him out* – but reason came back, and I said that I had to return to my flat to get some money, but it would only be 100 dollars. He asked again to enter with me, but I quipped: *"No, you wait here."* He ventured: *"How do I know you will come back?"* *"You have the gun,"* was my reply.

With a warning not to call the police because he knew where to find me, my corpulent gun-wielding *"amigo"* went away with a tenth of what he had demanded. He smiled, gave me a hug, and exclaimed: *"Thank you brother for your kindness!"* Incidentally, I did inform the Police, but they determined that there was not enough evidence, nor enough money involved, to pursue the matter. My assailant was arrested a week later during Sunday worship in a Baptist church in Tacna. His mistake was to brandish his gun at the pastor from the front pew without anticipating that two policemen, dressed in plain clothes, were worshipping there that day.

The reason I have recorded this, and similar episodes in my life is simply to emphasise something of my battle with sporadic anger. The theme I am following in this book is that of removing *"logs"* from my own eyes, and not that of seeking to help others until the Lord has helped me. I freely acknowledge that I have known many Christians who live as angry people. I see this as symptomatic of those who take hard-line stances regarding their biblical beliefs. I still do not warm to angry Christians. In fact, I do everything to avoid them.

Part of the desire to bless others is in learning to be on my guard against the presence of personal sin by taking it seriously, resisting it, and by fighting its power. To do so, the Holy Spirit, when called upon, gives power to overcome sin's control and to live a godlier life. Neither God nor the nature of the human heart has changed but God's Spirit breaks the chain of every sin that binds.

It is too easy to justify oneself by claiming to be in the right, while others are in the wrong. When inappropriately directed passions reign within us there are no limits or loyalties. Anger can be such a passion. It is not my responsibility to judge the wrath, or any other failing, in others, when I do not deal with my own problems. Furthermore, those who profess no faith in God represent a category that only God will finally judge. Once I repent, ask the Lord to forgive me and request the grace of God to remove the log from my eye, may I turn my attention to my brother and sister in Christ.

The biblical admonition is to *"gently and humbly help that person back onto the right path. And be careful not to fall into the same temptation yourself"* (Galatians 6:1b). Another Scripture that helps me is found in 1 Corinthians 5:12-13: *"[12] It isn't my responsibility to judge outsiders, but it certainly is your responsibility to judge those inside the church who are sinning. [13] God will judge those on the outside; but as the Scriptures say, 'You must remove the evil person from among you.'"*

PRAYER

Our God and Father I kneel again at the cross and remember that Christ died there for me. I stay there until I know afresh that but for your grace and mercy through Christ I could not be forgiven. My only boast is in Christ. In the light of that, help me to walk well with my brothers and sisters in Christ and to love both them and you as I ought. Amen

CHAPTER 4   **DEVOTIONS**

Since my earliest days of seeking to be a follower of Jesus Christ, I have treasured the Bible. I love the Scriptures and treat them as the inspired Word of God. When much younger I battled with how to study the Bible in the *"correct"* way. I even taught others how to do so. I finally settled on two basic approaches that I am comfortable with, and that *"work"* for me. This is especially so now that I am retired.

It is important to get a grip on any legalism related to personal devotions and the guilt that threatens to follow. Whereas I battled at different stages in life for balance, I came to enjoy my moments in fellowship with the Lord when I arrive at the discipline as fresh as I can. The schedule that best fits into my life is early in the morning when my mind is refreshed. My simple advice to people who are busy is to look for a space, free of other commitments, which might be at any point during the day.

There are two ways that guide me in my approach to the Bible. Firstly, I enjoy the panoramic methodology by reading through, over and over, from start to finish. The last time I read the entire Bible was during the first five months of 2021. This always gives me an overall perspective of God's Word and a few surprises along the way. Above all, the unity of both Testaments is on show regarding the nature of God and the central revelation of Christ in each separate book is there to be found.

Secondly, I engage in a microscopic and detailed study of biblical texts, where I take a few verses, set them in their context, and dig into them. This always results in Scripture giving up its treasures. Reading the script in different Bible versions, commentaries and other background aids gives way to putting questions to the text. Given that I believe the Bible to be the revelation of God, it is wise to start by asking what Scripture shows me about God himself.

The nature of God opens my eyes to the right and wrong way to live in the different situations of life. Faith in the Lord is always the way to face the difficulties and delights of life. This is the anchor that enables me to respond to variable human emotions and temptations that are there to overtake me daily. The realities of human life are addressed in the Bible.

The biggest challenge is to apply biblical truth in my own life here and now. At this point it leads to a process of meditating and praying as I bring to the Lord the tasks or pressures that lie ahead that day.

Meditation is basically the process of thinking everything through in the presence of God, whether at that moment, or during the day. This leads on inevitably to prayer, which is when I talk to the Lord about what I have studied.

Personal application comes first, and I suppose that until I pray the truth into my life, I have not truly studied the biblical text. One of the dangers for Bible teachers and preachers is to study Scripture with the goal of passing it on to others. That involves digging deeper to discover insights to relay in training and speaking. Over the years I am learning to separate my personal devotions from that other discipline. When I seek the Lord alone in Bible study and prayer, I discover that any additional motivation is not there to distract.

The way forward in all trying situations is the route of prayer. Anything bad, including times of ease and affluence that cause complacency, laziness, and the assumption that we are able of ourselves to cope with life by ourselves, potentially leads to forgetting our need of God. We must not let the heart stray after riches, or human pride. Neither suffering nor ease should find us without a suitable Christian response in prayer and praise.

Our faith in Jesus covers every experience. God invites us to come to him in everything. We have a God for all seasons, both in times of sufferings and blessings. God is our sufficiency. We hallow every pleasure, and we sanctify every pain. In praise, we thank God that his will is good. In times of trouble, it is for God's will that we pray. Prayer may not remove the suffering, but it can transform it. Always, the will of God is good.

The Bible is more concerned about God's providence than the exceptional acts of God. Miraculous happenings are not evenly spread through Scripture. Prayer for the sick belongs in every church. We thank God for medical science and for the providential goodness of God. God's sovereign hand is in control of all. There is no such thing as non-spiritual healing. We approach the doctor and God. Not all, but some sickness may be a punishment and a warning. Healing, in turn, involves the whole personality, whereby we desire to be fully reconciled to God.

Prayer is the peaceful acceptance of God's will. Faith goes hand in hand with the gift of faith; God is gracious to give the manifestation of faith in relation to something that we might ask for. It is always timely to remember the deceitfulness of the heart and the readiness to admit that we might be mistaken. Any predictions given to us by someone else in the name of God are open to honest tests. As we pray, we are committed to the will of God. The result is that true prayer requires us to wait and see what God might do. It does not depend on my will being done on earth but on God's so that little by little the Lord delivers us from insisting on being stubbornly right.

We may not get what we want just as soon as we pray. God is more concerned about our eternal salvation. The perfect will of God might be the lesser benefit of a return to bodily health, or in the supreme benefit of fullness of life in the immediate presence of Jesus. *"Thy will be done"* means we pray for what God has in mind because there is no more secure place than to leave matters in the hands of God.

When it comes to hearing someone's confession of sins, no one should hear another's admission of sin without the sole intention of making it a matter of prayer. We certainly need, if possible, to confess to the person against whom we have sinned, and from whom we need and desire to receive forgiveness. There is secret confession to God alone for secret sins. We also need to make public confession where applicable.

Where there is a breach in a fellowship, true penitence is required, with a spirit of reconciliation. Pride and fear can hold us back from sorting things out. A genuine spirit of prayer leads to healing. Corporate prayer expresses the need to undo damage to the individual and to the fellowship.

Biblical prayer directed to God through Christ is powerful, and it is effective when applied to human need. There is a spiritual foundation to prayer. This signifies that prayer is for ordinary people, who are prone to depression, in need of bravery and resolution, of fleeing from danger at other times, of being selfless in the concern for others, and of acknowledging being filled with self-pity at other times. This is the wonder of prayer, and the list goes on. Those who by the grace of God have been given a state of righteousness in his sight have been brought into the realm where effective prayer operates and have been given the right to exercise a ministry of prayer on behalf of others.

Supernatural results come from prayer learned in secret over the years. A mere person can move a God who answers prayer. Even when depressed a true Christian prays and experiences that it is good just to talk to God, and not to oneself. When a Christian truly prays the results that follow can only be produced by God. We just pray! Human prayer vies for divine results. One of the most useful practices is to mention everyday things to the Lord because all of life is lived with reference to him. In fact, there is no situation in which prayer is not the proper response.

There is no slick formula to prayer. Patience is what I have always been challenged to exhibit and experience in prayer. When the Lord has answered a prayer specifically that does not mean he will do so again in the same way. What that teaches me is simply that God can and does hear and respond. Thereafter, I know I can trust him.

I pray because I must. Prayer changes me, and the Lord shows me *"the logs"* that need to be removed as I place my hands in those of an unchangeable loving Father God. The Lord's solution to human need is what matters, and the faith that it is God's reply that counts. It is always his moment and not mine. My experience is that he alone can do far more than I ask and think (Ephesians 3:20).

One final lesson I am still learning is that there is no substitute for private devotions, no matter how faltering our efforts. No number of church meetings will ever substitute for the intimacy of seeking the Lord alone.

PRAYER

Heavenly Father thank you for the Scriptures and for the illumination that you give us through the Holy Spirit. Come, we ask, in power and bring new life to your church, renew us in love and service and enable us to be faithful to you our Lord and Master Jesus Christ as we seek to know you better and follow you more closely each succeeding day. Amen

CHAPTER 5   GETTING OLDER

Recently I read a statistical study of the world that concluded that only 8 percent of humanity live to exceed age 65. Given that I am 73 years old as I write this personal and diverse chapter, and in the light of the fact that 92 percent of the global population have left the world by 64 years of age, how can I not cherish life? On one level I take care of my health more than when younger and on the other I treasure every remaining moment as a gift from God.

When I was young, I was guilty at times of thinking that older people had always been that way. Perspectives came into the equation: in my teens, those in their twenties were getting on in life. Later, in my mid-twenties, forty was certainly not far from old age. When in my mid-forties, I well remember a businessman from the Crescent Church in Belfast, long since gone from the earth, saying, *"Ken, fifty is downhill, sixty is faster, and seventy, all the way!"* One sure thing is that seventy has come fast and for the last few years Jeannie and I have been saying to each other on our birthdays: *"How have we arrived here?"* Now, as I sit among older folk, I consider eighty to be old!

Jeannie and I have spent our lives placing our faith in the Lord and in his providential leading. Despite all the twists and turns of life, we came to not depend on money, security, and prestige for life, but in all that God promised to be for us in Christ. The Scottish scholar James Denney once stated that *"it is impossible at the same time to leave the impression .... that I am a great Christian, and that Jesus Christ is a great Master."* In the light of a perspective like that, we are challenged to seek to live for the glory of God each day.

The first major change that came with retirement in January 2014 was that I gave up my two part-time jobs. I was no longer the Postgraduate Studies Director in the Irish Baptist College or Mission Promoter in Baptist Missions. That meant I received no more wages from the Association of Baptist Churches in Ireland. I continued to lecture in the College, preach by invitation and travel to Peru. After retirement and up until 2019 the Mission Committee in Newtownbreda Baptist Church, instead of continuing sending support for me to Baptist Missions, recognised my ongoing role as an associate missionary of BM and agreed to pay my basic expenses on Peru visits. Without this I would not have been able to continue visiting the country I had come to love.

Several people encouraged me to keep on teaching and preaching and others said that there is nothing in the Bible about retirement! All good intentions aside, there are reasons why some of us should step out of certain ministries. Ecclesiastes chapter 12:1–7 makes it clear that age is not just a number and that it is wise to accept the maturing process. The biblical writer admonishes the reader to *"remember God in your youth before you grow old and say, 'Life is not pleasant anymore.'"* The author advises his readers several times to *"remember him [God] before..."* the advance of old age; a stage that includes waning eyesight, weakening legs and shoulders, tooth decay, fear of heights, lack of balance while walking, and diminishing energy and drive.

The above biblical references are accurate regarding growing older in a world without modern healthcare. With the passage of time an increasing number of us are sustained through a cocktail of pills. The wrinkles I observe on myself and on others of similar age indicate where smiles have been and are evidence of growing older. Having passed the nadir of middle age, I testify to never having been more content in life than now. An ideal day for me is to get up reasonably early, drink a leisurely cup of tea, read my Bible, and take my time to pray and meditate. Only afterwards do I drink my first cup of filter coffee along with Jeannie at breakfast. With family not too far away, what could be better? It is good that life has slowed up for us, much as we have.

I remember Father quoting Psalm 90, verses10 and 12 when referring to his advancing years: *"Seventy years are given to us. Some even live to eighty. But even the best years are filled with pain and trouble; soon they disappear, and we fly away.... Teach us to realize the brevity of life, so that we may grow in wisdom."* When he sensed his time came to die in May 1992, Mother informed me that during the last week of his life, he reaffirmed his faith in God by quoting Romans 10:9: *"If you confess with your mouth that Jesus is Lord and believe in your heart that God raised him from the dead, you will be saved."* After citing this Scripture, he stated on several occasions: *"That is what I believe."*

A sad part about life is when the person who gave us our memories, becomes a memory. I was not yet ready for my father to die. I remembered the good moments but regretted that I had not travelled to see him as his health failed and before there was no more time to be had. At that point, we had been in Northern Ireland for less than a year, after spending eighteen years in Peru as missionaries. I was finding it difficult to speak about our years in Peru in my lectures in the Belfast Bible College. That was a form of mourning. Simultaneously, the struggle to understand life in Northern Ireland was challenging. It was then, on return from a meeting in church one evening, that our fourteen-year-old son Samuel was waiting at our door to pass on the phone message he had received about Father's death.

Conclusions drawn from reading Scripture and by observing life enable a healthy focus regarding death. The brevity of life puts paid to any boasting about oneself. We cannot presume to continue alive at will. It is audacity to think that we are masters of our own lives so that what we must do is decide and lo and behold it all happens. This idea is too prevalent in our society where we are given the mantra that we will succeed just because we will it. Jeannie and I constantly thank God that there is more to life than making money or *"doing well"* as life's sole objective. The heart of the matter is the will of God. That we can do nothing without God's permission is such an important realization and is a healthy antidote to human pride.

Christians who have allowed financial power to turn their heads often remain blind to the fact that Christ is Lord of all. Worldly wealth has too frequently hardened hearts against brothers and sisters less amply provided for. As the people of God, we draw comfort from the Scripture as we watch, wait, and remain faithful. We are called to a life that pleases God as he entrusts resources to us to use as an adjunct to seek to walk humbly with God.

There are down-to-earth indications of aging. These include struggling to remember people's names, feeling stiffer, spending time comparing illnesses and injuries with friends, avoiding lifting heavy things due to back concerns, struggling to lose weight easily, falling asleep in front of the TV most evenings, needing an afternoon nap, not knowing any songs in the top ten, misplacing glasses/bag/car keys/etc., getting more hairy (ears, eyebrows, nose, face, etc.), hating noisy places, choosing clothes and shoes for comfort rather than for style, thinking policemen/teachers look really young, saying *"it wasn't like that when I was young,"* finding we have no idea what *"young people"* are talking about, having colleagues who are so young they do not know what a cassette tape is, complaining about the rubbish on television these days, not knowing or remembering the name of any modern bands, moving from Radio 1 to Radio 2 (actually, I listen to Classic FM), losing touch with everyday technology such as tablets and TVs, buying a smart phone but having no idea how to do anything other than make phone calls on it (my granddaughter Anjali, who is nine years old, teaches me), feeling we have the right to tell people exactly what we are thinking, even if it isn't polite (well, my mother did!), being told off for politically incorrect opinions and, to cap it all, our ears are getting bigger! The list goes on!

I am sure now that each new generation, in youth, finds it hard to make sense of the older one or even wants to belong to it. After the milestone of passing their driving test young people are off and away. I guess the hardest part is to accept, with grace, that we have moved into another stage in life. Jeannie and I went on a visit to Orkney in 2019 and a younger person, whose identity I will take to the grave, commented on my two older brothers Robert and Ivan, 74 and 72 respectively at the time, as they were trying to catch sheep. *"They think they are as young as ever, but they look like two old men staggering about[21]."*

Losing one's memory is the biggest worry about getting old and, sadly, many of us have witnessed loved ones being *"lost"* to spouses and families years before death. A secondary concern is about the impact aging will have on physical fitness. Loneliness in old age is a concern for those who become isolated, very evident during recent lockdowns. The fear of losing good looks takes precedence for others. This is especially sad when a person never possessed what is considered attractiveness in the first place! My struggles with technology not only indicate that I am getting on a bit but also feature as a determining factor in my decision-making process.

Lockdowns during the Covid-19 pandemic have served me as a time to reflect on all the above. This leads me to articulate just a very few of my thoughts about getting older. My memories of pre-schools years recall the contentment of being alone. While not an antisocial being I have always enjoyed the challenge of working out my assignments as something of a loner. This changed from too casual an approach to study during my secondary education, to the challenge of being given lone responsibilities on the farm (1966-1968). A favourite task was walking around the fields making sure the sheep were fine.

In my final year of studies in the Birmingham Bible Institute (1968-1971) I at last began to enjoy studying. Something simply clicked, I approached study seriously, and my marks soared to a new level. During the same period, the truth that God has no favourites and makes no distinctions[22] was not always evident in the behaviour of some fellow

---

[21] I just could not resist including that.
[22] See Colossians 3:25c.

students when they were elected as student representatives. It seemed to go to their heads and resulted in a self-importance previously absent.

Friends begged me to accept their nomination to be a student candidate for that all-important committee. Although my decision caused considerable ire, I did not let my name go forward. I was more-than-happy to allow another friend, John Faulkner, be the sole nominee. It was not that I was not on other committees as I oversaw the children's outreach team at BBI for over two years. That was enough for me at the time. I trace my aversion to board meetings from that time. It puzzled me why self-importance came so readily to those elected.

This same conviction followed me into a stint as pastor in Orkney (1971-1973), assistant pastor in Edinburgh, first term in Peru as a missionary (1975-1978), and when elected as field leader for the Regions Beyond Missionary Union, firstly in late 1981. I suppose I owe my terminology to the part-time and full-time postgraduate study of new religious movements in the University of Aberdeen (1978-1979; 1980-1981; 1985-1988). I simply call autocracy and the accompanying narcissism a *"little big man"* complex. It seemed wrong to carry the nomenclature of Field Director, in any team, where each person is just one among equals.

It has always looked to me to be an affront to God that elitism and autocratic behaviour should exist among Christians. It is hard to see this as simply amiable weaknesses. My happiest time in the Regions Beyond Missionary Union (RBMU later amalgamated into Latin Link) was when sharing the executive committee with colleagues like Ray Miller, David Stevens, and Cherry Noble. All of this is simply an explanation of why I have never really been happy as a *"committee man."* This is not intended to be a justification for my attitude, but the identification of a *"log"* that needed to change.

I have never been more contented than when overseeing a project. In later missionary experience it was more than being a lone worker or of not revelling in committees. I suppose it was part of being a field-missionary and my amusement at what I have termed *"little big men."* Previously, on the family farm I was just one of the workers when there was a task that required several to be involved. Incompetence was not uncommon in a mission context, and I had seen this taken to its logical conclusion with the dismissal of personnel based on their laziness. Into that personal mix I discovered that a joy in togetherness leads to balance.

Harmonious Christian fellowship of believers in Christ is the soil out of which grows the whole life that pleases God.

The biggest bonus of having been a missionary for so many years is having had my eyes opened to a wider world through cultural experiences. Appreciation of the Majority World[23] is fatal to prejudice, bigotry, and narrow mindedness. Meeting other cultures and expressions leads me to appreciate and to remember that we are all different. The mysteries of life disappear in the light of that, and life stands better explained. Also, when travelling with other people, it is not long before one finds out what they are really like.

Opinionated, stubborn, narrow-minded, self-conceited attitudes are *"the logs"* in life that need to change. It has always seemed sad that the many splits and divisions among Christians produce a supermarket of churches on a world scale. I observe growth in some *"contemporary"* churches at the expense of and the demise of others. While those who join them are lauded, those who leave are questioned about their theology and their motives!

Despite our inability to practise fellowship with brothers and sisters in Christ, faith in the sovereignty of national churches, whatever label is attached, is basic. Many such churches experience their initial growth through foreign and national pioneers to increase numerically into that of self-governing, self-propagating, and self-supporting national entities. That is the ideal. It is a backward step when the founders are almost deified, and change is rejected. On the other hand, a great variety of churches become like conveyor belts. While new members enter through the front door others exit within years through another.

The sovereignty of the Church over those who minister within it is not in question. Recognizing that as a missionary our task is to serve and to be subject to a church is healthy. I believe that, in the Lord's good pleasure, he gave me the vision for a diversity of projects over recent decades. I learned after years of ministry in Peru to no longer be involved in too many ministries. It cost my family a heavy price. It seemed wiser to dedicate my effort to one *"new"* effort at one given time.

---

[23] Majority World is a less pejorative term than Third World. This is especially so in the light of the sophistication present in large swathes of our planet where the human population exceeds that of the West.

Each project started with prayer, continued with a vision statement and plan, which led into raising funds for, and the implementation of each succeeding ministry. It was a joy to fulfil the vision through human and material resources. The idea was always to move on and to hand things on. There is a right time to do so. I confess that it was especially difficult when I sensed that folk, who did not always share the same original vision, nor had expended much effort, were new to the task, then jostled for a position. More than once, in retrospect, I pulled out before the project had been sufficiently established. This was due to either trusting the wrong people, or by moving too fast, and then by living to regret it.

I learned from colleagues in my earliest days in Peru the art of not holding on to a position because of self-interest or of misguided ideas of self-importance. By that stage I had pretty much come to dislike labels. I was, and am, an interdenominational Christian, and enjoy the privilege of working with people from different church backgrounds. Regarding ministry, it is important to know when to step back. When I asked a retired church elder, whom I deeply respect, about the over seventies in up-front ministry in a church, he simply replied: *"It would result in young people steering away."* In their desire to satisfy its members, churches that offer both *"traditional"* and *"contemporary"* services on Sundays may simply be accentuating divisions that already exist.

By the time I reached Peru as a missionary in 1974 I was convinced of my gifting as an evangelist. After a stint as a pastor and assistant pastor in Scotland, I was *"cured"* of seeking a purely pastoral ministry. In my young zeal I was prepared for trekking over mountainous terrain at altitude. One such high-risk hike with a short-term worker called Bryan Twedell, that lasted all the daylight hours available to us, still gives me nightmares when I think about it. That was then. I travelled too much here and there and did not dedicate enough energy to local ministry.

"Decisions" for Christ came fast and furious. However, it was not long before I knew I needed to develop a ministry of Bible teaching. This led on to real fulfilment in life as lecturer and as administrator, firstly in Peru, and then in the Belfast Bible College. When it came to developments in technology, I have consistently remained a few steps behind everyone!

I have sought, over the years, to steer a middle path regarding my theological stance. When first elected as field coordinator in Peru, as I preferred to call my role, I learned a lot from delving into the central mission files in Peru. Be careful what you write! There were records regarding my candidacy as a missionary where I was categorized as exhibiting a Pentecostal theology. This was viewed as negative. The adage that adverse news travels thousands of miles while the truth does not travel more than a mile, comes to mind.

I had already paid a price in my home church, and had been told by others, in no uncertain times, that such ideas regarding the ongoing existence of the gifts of the Spirit were not of God. By the time I arrived in Peru, I was also dubbed a *"rebel"* because I had met Jeannie in Costa Rica and got engaged to her without informing or asking permission from those above me in RBMU! That was all on file. I admit that my heart had taken me on a journey with her, that led to our marriage in the USA on December the 28th in 1974, for which permission was finally granted by the last resistance from the Peru field committee.

What really came as a shock was a subsequent split in RBMU. The Americans in RBMU insisted on a tight doctrinal statement, the non-admittance of Pentecostals and Charismatics and on the parity of Mission and Church government. British RBMU members welcomed interdenominational Christians, with varied secondary beliefs, and held to the sovereignty of the national church over any para-ecclesiastic organization seconded to it. Jeannie was American and came over to the British!

A constant trauma for me was to hold to my secondary beliefs, which I sought to keep close to my chest and guard as personal convictions, so as not to be misjudged, while pursuing fellowship with all others who trusted Jesus Christ for salvation. I have practised living my life accordingly and have continued to dislike the labels used to define individual Christians and their church affiliations.

Nothing has tested me more in my desire to be a Christian. Not even sickness, cancer in the family, financial concerns, relative poverty, or a decade of terrorism in Peru caused me more pain. I expect those who do not believe in the Lord to give me grief. However, when it comes to those in the church, it has been pure hard work to employ diplomacy among Christians to avoid division. My father always taught by example to identify and to seek fellowship with anyone who testified to faith in Christ. That has been my objective.

When years of perceived issues relating to significant Christian autocratic leadership, evidence of *"silly and polarised"* outworking of Scripture, the presence of nepotism, *"bullying/controlling"* preaching, *"stealing"* other church members, and exaggerated pleas for money are included, something finally gave way in me. In the light of a reaction to the above apparent Christian behaviour I also came to loathe any scenario where people who were not present at a given time were discussed negatively. This included what happened in committees.

Traumas vary in nature and given that they may be accumulative I suffered from severe panic attacks in 2011. I was desperate enough to ask for an appointment with Principal Edwin Ewart[24] of the Irish Baptist College. His advice was simple: *"Go to the doctor."* I will always be grateful to him for that counsel. What followed, once clinical depression had been eliminated as a condition, were fourteen weeks of Cognitive Behavioural Therapy. The female psychiatrist coaxed me into writing down a list of my thoughts that led to panic attacks. I found that easy. Her observation made me prick up my ears and understand in a new way: *"If I had all those thoughts[25] in my head at any one time, I too would have a panic attack."*

The therapist examined my negative thoughts associated with multiple life-traumas as she sought to replace them with positive ones. It was when she explained the technical meanings of mindfulness and perspectives in the context of therapy that I gained an understanding of what made me ruminate on distressing experiences. I was encouraged to comprehend those images, thoughts, places, which could trigger anxiety and that needed to be seen in a new light. The hyper vigilance that led to being constantly on the alert for potential threats to my convictions, at times had caused emotional detachment and, occasionally, a feeling of being numb. In turn, the defensiveness led to a measure of short temper, to mild depression, and to panic.

There are several memories from my earliest days when folk would mention, in whispered tones, of people who suffered from their *"nerves."* Those who hurt in that way were given the therapy of the day while those on the outside never seemed to understand that it required more than giving themselves *"a good shake"* and simply getting on with life. I would never want to minimize the magnitude of other people's trauma, so now, with a wish to be honest, I reluctantly share some of mine. I express my hesitancy because I regret having shared my

---

[24] I do not include Pastor Edwin Ewart in any of the appraisals articulated in the text. My time in the Irish Baptist College (2008-2014) was a happy time.
[25] She used an expletive. I substituted the word *"poo"* to ask her if that was what she meant!

struggles with people who simply dismissed them or, worse still, brought them up again, as if to punish.

Although I mention 2011 as a time when I suffered panic attacks, I had experienced some sporadically over the years. I keep those to myself. So, when I, for the first time in my life, sought help, it was because I felt devastated, convulsed, and shamed. I was having a crisis of faith because, if I had asked the Lord for help once, I had asked a thousand times, to no avail. This resulted in emotions of shame and helplessness.

When I eventually pursued closure, I knew I had to confront the truth. Help was slow in coming and only began to happen when I made space and did not run away. I was given expert advice that because I had developed diabetes type 2 fluctuations in sugar levels could affect physical and mental wellbeing. Without fully realizing what I was doing I began to walk and felt the benefits. The distances increased and I now invest in walking shoes instead of the gym! Writing is a therapy and is my way of handling distant traumas that require healing. This book is an expression of truth, intended for trusted friends, and not for those outside that circle.

Jeannie and I moved to St Patrick's Drumbeg Church of Ireland in early 2020. We were introduced to a man gifted as a pastor in the person of the Rector, Rev Willie Nixon. We have enjoyed ministry in the Word of God and in the Spirit there since then. Early on in this transition Rev Willie shared Proverbs 16:9 with me: *"We can make our plans, but the Lord determines our steps."* Our interdenominational experiences up until then easily determined *"our steps."* Issues of concern for us were recognized, good questions were asked of us, and we felt that our answers were welcomed. It was good to be listened to, and to experience our need of acceptance.

On a very human level the myth of being able to continue the same as before into old age had taken a knock. Confidence in oneself and in the Lord had always been challenged by the anomalies of conflicting Christian profession and behaviour. It was much more than the ever-increasing limitations of aging. I was progressively gratified that I could answer searching challenges by admitting I did not know the answer. To be out of my depth was fine. It came as a relief to be true to myself when I could acknowledge freely to having met true Roman Catholic and Seventh Day Adventist believers in Jesus Christ on my travels. This did not elicit a near-violent counterattack.

A conviction had grown in me over many years that there is a biblical rationale to have faith in the Lord and at the same time to meet human needs. This holistic view extends to all the care ministries. It had been too easy to attribute such *"social help"* to *"liberal Christians."* There is new joy in supporting charities and in being active by helping people for no other reason than that there is a need for aid. Every call to be agents of change in our world is for every single child of God. The Apostle Paul writes in 1 Corinthians 15:58: *"Always work enthusiastically for the Lord, for you know that nothing you do for the Lord is ever useless."*

Before I run away with thoughts of replacing the Good News of Jesus' Kingdom, I wish to include a quotation from 1 Corinthians 9: 15-16:

> *[15] In fact, I would rather die than lose my right to boast about preaching without charge. [16] Yet preaching the Good News is not something I can boast about. I am compelled by God to do it. How terrible for me if I didn't preach the Good News.*

Implicit in the text is Paul's disdain for gaining money from his preaching and the inner drive that leads true children of God to share their faith. This has guided me to question the accumulation of wealth by several tele-evangelists[26], of Executive Directors of Christian charities, and of some pastors to be paid exorbitant wages. How can we do otherwise than present Jesus to people? In articulating this, Paul is dismissing the false nature of so-called prosperity theology, insidiously present today, whether explicit or implicit.

Missionary involvement in the Majority World has changed over the years. The task for western missionaries is not restricted to proclaiming Christ and to Church planting. What I write here represents a lifetime of reflections. Too many books, authors, colleagues, students, and cultural experiences have shaped my thinking for me to be able to acknowledge them all. I simply articulate my conclusions as I view things now.

Most interdenominational agencies are crying out for candidates who have many kinds of spiritual gifts as well as academic and practical training that can set free evangelists, church planters, and Bible teachers so that they, together with national church leaders can make disciples of Jesus Christ. Administrators, teachers of missionary children, medical personnel, language teachers, trades people, and other professionals, are greatly needed.

---

[26] This is easy to check out online!

There was a time in my life in 1991 that major change came to challenge me in the form of the amalgamation of RBMU and the Evangelical Union of South America to form Latin Link (LL). Shift can be painful, especially if we become comfortable with how things are. I was relaxed with where we were at in RBMU at that time. Now, with the advantage of hindsight, LL is the kind of entity that I could join, again!

After formation in 1991, there was an initial thrust to serve in contemporary Latin mission through *"partnership in mission"* and this developed, in time, to *"community with a calling."* Service to growing Latin churches varies from a range of part time programmes[27] to long term *"Stay"* plans. Direction for LL moved from the West to Latin America. Leadership, and decisions at the cutting edge are taken by missionaries in their personal ministries and by those appointed to different departments. There is a two-way traffic as Latins travel, on a basis of parity with western missionaries to other countries, and those from the West to Latin America. The concept of operating under the sovereignty of national churches undergirds all the projects.

On my twelfth visit back to Peru in April 2015, after having left *"for good"* in September 2007, I had a memorable experience. By the time I reached Dallas on American Airlines flight number 370 on Monday 6th April at 8.41pm, I was weary from a long day as I had travelled from Belfast via Dublin and Philadelphia. On my connecting flight number AA980 scheduled to depart at 10.22pm, I met a LL team of elderly widows[28], accompanied by their leader. Between departure from Dallas and arrival in Lima on the 7th of April at 5.22am, I recall the enthusiasm of the six ladies as they robbed me of sleep by outlining what they were to do on their LL short-term project in Arequipa, Peru.

The Latin Link International Director, Paul Turner, met them in Lima and later updated me on the success of that project. I knew that I had witnessed the pure joy and anticipation of Christian widows from an Anglican church in England of taking part in mission. I have no doubt that short-term involvement of that nature leads to knock-on effects on

---

[27] Short term programmes vary from 6-24 months and include serving in a cross-cultural Latin American mission setting. Medical electives, Spanish or Portuguese university study alongside a Christian-run project, a cross-cultural placement for Bible college students, or sabbaticals for individuals in a mission setting are just some of the options to choose from.
[28] Age is relative as I was only 66 years of age at the time. The ladies were all over seventy!

those who participate, on the local believers in Latin America, and on sending churches in the West.

However, I wish to add one cautionary comment based on personal experiences and observation. Sending churches and mission agencies need to be sure to have in place careful debriefing, follow-up, and counselling. Things do not always turn out well for everyone. Professional help should not be an afterthought.

Many *"logs"* have had to be got rid of so that, for the first time in my life, I am finally ready to formulate my views, as they are now, on a different and most difficult topic. I articulate the issue that I constantly encountered on my travels by identifying the centrality of a gospel that appears at times to elevate physical healing to the level of repentance and faith in Jesus Christ. It is an understatement to declare this to have been an area of much confusion, polarization, silly behaviour by Christians, insensitive outworking, heart searching and personal pain.

Scripture speaks of two distinct and equally real afflictions, that of diseases and of demons. Jesus rebukes fevers, by the touch of his hand he heals, he cures people's ills by a word, and demons came out at his command. Jesus' power takes immediate effect in the biblical accounts, and he often insists on doing so quietly, without the beneficiary making any fuss. Jesus is the same today! That is beyond doubt.

I have prayed for many sick people and know that it is not simply a matter of either the miraculous or the medical, but that healing is something much deeper than that. It is my continued observation that it is never as easy as us replicating a command such as *"in the name of Jesus be healed."* Well-meaning Christians continue to do so and assign both diseases and demons to hell *"in Jesus' name."* If only that were so!

Meanwhile, Jesus, who is the same today may choose to do something more far-reaching, to be of greater benefit in the long run. What he does may be more protracted and more painful. He knows how to treat disorders of which we may not be aware. Jesus deals with the needs of the whole person and not only the obvious needs. His aim may be to calm the spirit, to give courage, or to clarify a vision. Jesus knows what he is doing. Healing, as such, may not be experienced in this life, but at the final day[29].

---

[29] 1 Corinthians 15:53: *"For our dying bodies must be transformed into bodies that will never die; our mortal bodies must be transformed into immortal bodies."*

Words in Scripture carry double meanings so that the same term for salvation can mean to heal, or another signifies to raise from sickness and to raise from death. All those healed in the time of Jesus, later died, even Lazarus, who was raised from death. The prayer of faith (James 5:15) cannot fail to bring about the result, one way or the other. The prayer of trust goes beyond the way we advise the Lord to act. Our faith is in Jesus the healer, who will choose his own timing and method.

When it comes to giving pastoral counsel, I thank God for wise Christian leaders who know when they are out of their depth. To realize where help is available and to point someone in that direction is wise. This is especially so when seeking to support people who, for example, suffer from alcohol and drug addiction. There are conditions that require doctors and specialists who are trained to diagnose, make a prognosis and to prescribe remedies.

Pastoral care is the one quality that, when absent, unmasks the reality of all Bible teachers and spiritual leaders. Too many aspire to up-front ministry but shy away from the down-to-earth nature of shepherding God's people. For instance, I have listened to many sermons on idolatry. In one series I waited in vain for a clear biblical explanation, so much so, that by the end, I was convinced that idols were being so invented, that the hearer could only feel guilty about almost everything. To follow Christ is made obvious by placing no one and nothing in the place of loving God, and this, in turn, is evident in its practical outworking in our love for the people and things that surround us.

The Apostle Paul's admonition in Ephesians 5:3 is clear: *"Let there be no sexual immorality, impurity, or greed among you. Such sins have no place among God's people."* Paul indicates that none of those who live like that *"will inherit the Kingdom of Christ and God."* I have listened to the denunciation of sexual immorality and impurity; I am still waiting for Paul's conclusion to the same passage being quoted in this context. He writes: *"For a greedy person is an idolater, worshipping the things of this world"* (Ephesians 5:5). What is confusing is to hear a denunciation of Christians seeking success and material goods in a sermon, followed by the clause, *"but of course there is nothing wrong with that!"*

THE FINAL LAP

On Channel Four News I listened recently to a top official from the United Nations explaining some consequences from the war in the Ukraine[30]. From the incursion into the Ukraine alone, up to one billion more people will be driven into abject poverty. Conflict, climate change, and Covid-19[31] exacerbate the situation and precipitate an increase in refugees, terrorism and human trafficking, social tragedies already present in our world. It remains to be seen how world events will encroach more on our daily lives.

It was one thing to live in Peru in a context where we were faced daily with the double realities of the very rich and the very poor. It is quite something else to live in the West where this is not yet the case to that extent. The danger here is to encounter a presentation of the Christian faith that accepts the possibility of forgiveness without requiring repentance, without confession, without discipleship, without the cross, without Jesus Christ, living and incarnate. True biblical grace confronts us as a merciful call to follow Jesus, it is a word of forgiveness to the broken spirit, and to the contrite heart. It is costly as we bow to the yoke of Christ and follow him; it is a blessing because Jesus says: *"My yoke is easy, and my burden is light."*

The final state is directly related to the present life and what we have done for Christ and, more importantly, what we have allowed Christ to do through us and in us by his Spirit. Scripture teaches that heaven is ours' solely because we have washed our robes *"in the blood of the Lamb"* (Revelation 22:10-14). In the Bible, death signifies the continuation of personal life but in a changed state. The Old Testament looked forward to a glory after death[32]. Heaven will become an unimaginable life with Christ at a new level *"which would be far better for me"* (Philippians 1:23) than living here on earth.

---

[30] I took down copious notes as Channel Four aired their interview. Just before I wrote this summary, Rebecca's dog, Oscar, managed to chew up my handwritten record. I succeeded in rescuing enough to outline a brief appraisal in the text.
[31] Some might argue that Brexit has made its distinct contribution to the worsening situation in the U.K.!
[32] Psalm 73:24: *"You guide me with your counsel, leading me to a glorious destiny."*

Lord Jesus Christ you are everything I need. If you are not the centre of my affection, of my worship, of my life, if I do not remember that all is for you Lord Jesus, have mercy on me and forgive me. Your Father, and now my father wanted you Lord to be first in everything. Help me to make it so in my life.

Heavenly Father, at times we are way out of our depths. Take our minds, we pray, and enable us to understand your Word, take our hearts and fill us with love for you and for everyone. Place Jesus in the highest place in all our ambitions so that we might know him and the power of his resurrection. Amen

CHAPTER 6   LOOKING AFTER ONESELF

This short chapter includes a few costly practical lessons learned over decades through self-scrutiny. The application of biblical tests to my life and ministry led to *"getting rid of logs."* Study of the Word of God quickly shows whether one's perceived calling is compatible with its teaching. In short, when I travelled to Peru in 1974, I firmly believed my gifting was that of an evangelist. Over the years I began to develop other avenues of service as priorities. A Bible teaching ministry was next in the chronological sequence.

This led, in time to great satisfaction in a more administrative role, firstly, in Peru, then in the Belfast Bible College and later in the Irish Baptist College. Along the way, when on study leave, I was employed as a pastor, on another occasion in Scotland on a farm, and in the USA on construction sites. Manual work has always been gratifying and especially when bread was needed on the table. I found great joy in making sure Baptist Missions had adequate Peruvian administration in place, oversaw various projects, and acted as project manager in the construction of numerous buildings. Discussion with trusted Christian friends and advisers confirmed each new next step along the way.

I know that I am not alone when I indicate the human need for time out and for the possibility of the now-famous state of being burned out. I never quite reached that point but testify to being *"browned out."* Prior to caring for others, we must look after ourselves. Paul gives counsel to the leaders of the Ephesian church in Acts 20:28: *"So guard yourselves and God's people. Feed and shepherd God's flock – his church, purchased with his own blood – over which the Holy Spirit has appointed you as elders."* Paul's advice is to look after *"yourselves"* first, and then God's people in the church.

There is a biblical path to Christian maturity with a promise of a crown to those who love God and go along the route of endurance (James 1:25). The road to blessing is through hearing and doing the Word of God. A constant challenge in my walk with the Lord is to know that I am experiencing the Lord's grace. It is not easy to point others to the way of life unless I tread the road of obedience myself. Self-examination leads me to ask myself what my life with God is like at any given time.

> *To the end that we should always remember the exceeding great love of our Master, and only Saviour, Jesus Christ, thus dying for us, and the innumerable benefits which by his precious*

blood-shedding he hath obtained to us; he hath instituted and ordained holy mysteries, as pledges of his love, and for a continual remembrance of his death, to our great and endless comfort. (The Book of Common Prayer)

At the end of Revelation Jesus is the coming one (22:20) who says, *"yes, I am coming soon!"* He who declared the message of salvation in those far-off days will soon return to complete his work and take his ransomed saints home to heaven. In the meantime, he is the giver of grace (22:21), who cheers and strengthens his expectant people by bringing home to them the living power of both the message to which they look back and of the hope to which they look forward. This blessing is a tonic for hard times to all who are prepared to take to heart *"this revelation from Jesus Christ, which God gave him to show to his servants...God blesses the one who reads"* (Revelation 1:1, 3).

There is difference between serving the Lord with zeal from making sure that we stay in for the long haul. Just as in the case of any soldier, we who are in a spiritual battle, can be battle-scarred. God wants us to survive and flourish as we seek to mature in the faith. Maintaining a healthy body, mind, and spirit are all aspects of knowing God. God begins and completes a good work in us and encourages us to *"be transformed by the renewing of our mind"* (Romans 12:2).

Good spiritual health requires a decent grounding in doctrine, the Scriptures, prayer, worship, reading, quiet times, frequent attendance at the Lord's Table, practising God's presence in our lives, maintaining good interpersonal relationships in church and with other people. Flexibility, and the will to grow are key to progress in a personal friendship with the Lord, but there is nothing unspiritual about learning alternative patterns.

Starting off as healthy as possible is aided by consulting professionals about physical and mental health. Steps may be taken to improve wellbeing, and to maintain it. Decent eating habits, exercise patterns, enlarging one's mind, are all sensible. Good health depends on cleaning up old excess emotional baggage where any bitterness, jealousy, hatred, anger, resentment, feelings of inferiority, and so on, may linger. Help should be sought if any of this causes persistent trouble.

If one starts with an overload of issues, then these may escalate in the service of God. My observations of experiences in another culture over several decades highlight common reactions to change. After an initial honeymoon period, culture shock may or may not develop. In every experience of difference, fatigue, disliking the place, people, job, food, church, mission, may be the result. This in turn might grow into homesickness, depression, anxiety, and anger.

Treatment for a Christian begins by asking the Lord for patience, as things may pass and tend to improve. It helps to be kind to yourself without accusing self of false guilt. More rest and the enjoyment of a few treats can go a long way. At times, just a small piece of Scripture that brings calm is worth holding on to. Then there is the comfort of talking with real friends.

How do we aid staying well as we follow Christ? Care for the body includes, as already mentioned, a healthy diet. Common sense dictates that injections should be kept up to date. It is often wise to follow local rest patterns in hot climates. Adequate time off, plus ample work drive militates against either laziness or becoming a workaholic. There is a delicate balance between the two.

When it comes to caring for the mind habits already learned in life can be expanded. Wide reading is positive as well as a study of any local area. Keeping in touch with family, providing relationships are good, is always a bonus. Besides enrolling in study courses, which in my case, ended up with four university degrees, I learned to respect *"small"* service for God. God does not despise the minuscule. Jesus taught that we should pray, give alms, fast, or whatever, in secret and not to be seen. Too many Christians feel their public contribution is of the essence. May I add that a smile at people goes a long way. Be nice! There is never an excuse for rudeness!

Human interactions are to be cultivated through respect for other people. The list goes on relative to other expatriates, host nationals, colleagues, husbands, wives, children, and difficult individuals. Why are they like that? As I grow older, I attempt to talk things over! Prayer and mutual forgiveness play their parts. Incidentally, I have found it useful to ask if I am also problematic! True friends will be honest. Avoidance of inappropriate opposite sex relationships should be avoided as much as friendships of an exclusive nature.

Our bond to God through Christ is paramount. This is the one area that it takes time to develop. I expect to grow in my knowledge and understanding of the Lord as I spend time with him. To do so there is no short cut. Advice given to me early in life to keep short accounts with

God and to be square with him every day is important. *"New every morning are the mercies of God"* is so true. I am still learning that if I am exhausted, the Lord is not bothered if my prayers, my worship, and my Bible readings are short!

Accepting the responsibility for the load the Lord wants me to carry is where everything comes together. So many *"logs"* have had to be ditched in my life. The balance between taking on too much or taking on too little is where sanctified common sense comes in. When in a position of authority, the appropriate approach is to delegate where applicable. What is my personal load? Avoidance of taking on too much permanently means perhaps examining what can be dropped. Guilty feelings of *"oughtness"* are not the basis for guidance. If there is the contemplation for more, as a rule, talk it over with friends and the Lord!

PRAYER

Lord Jesus Christ, I pray that your kingdom will rule and that your presence will be in my heart, and in all who profess to know and love you. Enrich me with your presence Lord. Help me to live in a way that is worthy of the Gospel. I want so to live that other people will see, hear, understand, and come to know you our Lord and Saviour and that all the glory will result in being given to you. I pray in the Almighty name of the Lord Jesus Christ. Amen

CHAPTER 7 WHAT YOU SEE IS WHAT YOU GET

"Each time he said, 'My grace is all you need. My power works best in weakness.' So now I am glad to boast about my weaknesses, so that the power of Christ can work through me" (2 Corinthians 12:9).

The Apostle Paul discovered, in a dramatic real-life situation, that God's power is brought to us in our weakness, not in our strength. Other so-called apostles were boasting of being more spiritual than he was because of their visions and experiences. What is new! Their so-called revelations from God were presented as their credentials to the church in Corinth. Paul rejects this as false.

The debate between power and weakness is still with us today, believe me. In fact, although Paul had, fourteen years previously, a *"third heaven"* experience (vs. 1-4), his credentials are not on display in power, but in the down-to-earth reality of weakness, lived out before his fellow believers. Paul was simply stating that *"what you see is what you get."* He writes in verse 6: *"...I don't want anyone to give me credit beyond what they see in my life or hear in my message...."*

It was precisely because Paul had really met with God fourteen years previously that he could write that. He made no claim to be a *"super-apostle."* Although God had called him to be an apostle, he termed himself the least of them all, when he wrote to the same church in AD 56 (1 Cor. 15:9). *"Such wonderful revelations from God are not a matter of boasting but of humility."* Paul writes in verse 6: *"I will boast only about my weaknesses."*

Paul was led to this truth when *"a thorn in his flesh"* was given to him by Satan (v. 7) *"to torment"* him and keep him *"from becoming proud."* In his pain Paul asked the Lord three times to remove the *"thorn."* Many have attempted to explain the nature of the thorn, but Scripture is silent. What we do know is that the Lord spoke to Paul's heart about his grace through weakness.

The *"thorns"* in life may remain with us, whatever they may be. At times we, like Paul, learn to leave them with God. The pain is real and debilitating, just as it was for Paul. This is not just a nice devotional thought. The eternal truth of God is that in some mysterious way his plan is that while our present existence may be dogged by sin and suffering, his grace draws us closer to Christ, as he says to us, *"My grace is all you need. My power works best in weakness."*

Jesus asked his Heavenly Father several times in the Garden of Gethsemane that the *"cup"* of suffering be removed from him. Imagine, if God had answered that prayer there would have been no atoning death on the cross and no *"grace to help in time of need."*

Pardon is at the heart of the gospel, but it is not the whole doctrine of grace. The New Testament sets God's gift of pardon in the context of a plan of salvation that began with election before the world was and will be completed only when the church is perfect in glory. Its fullest account is in the massive original paragraph running from Ephesians 1:3 to 2:10.

The promises of God will stand and be fulfilled. Grace will be shown to be sovereign. In Christ we have redemption through his blood, the forgiveness of sins, in accordance with the riches of God's grace that he lavished on us (Ephesians 1:7-8).

The idea that retribution might be the moral law of God's world and an expression of the holy character of God seems to us quite fantastic. Yet the Scriptures insist throughout that the world that God in his goodness has made is a moral realm, one in which retribution is as basic a fact as breathing. God is the judge of all the earth, and God is not true to himself unless he punishes sin. Unless one knows and feels the truth of this fact that wrongdoers have no natural hope of anything from God but retributive judgement, one can never share the biblical faith in divine grace.

It was Malcolm Muggeridge who stated: *"The depravity of man is at once the most empirically verifiable reality but at the same time the most resisted fact."*

Are we not tempted to have too high an opinion of ourselves? We dismiss a bad conscience, in ourselves as in others, as an unhealthy psychological freak, a sign of disease and mental aberration rather than an index of moral reality. We are convinced that, despite all our *"little sins"* we are at heart thoroughly good folks. Our world consistently trades being good and doing good for looking good or feeling good.

It is too easy to imagine God as a magnified image of ourselves and assume that God shares our own complacency about ourselves. The very thought that we might be fallen creatures from God's image, rebels against God's rule, guilty and unclean in God's sight, fit only for God's condemnation, may never enter our heads. And without this understanding of sin, we miss our desperate need of grace.

Christians still tend to have a league table of gifts, prizing the more dramatic above the more ordinary. Spiritual gifts are essential for every church and the most excellent way of discovering them is through love (1 Corinthians 13). The less excellent way is through an unhealthy desire to be a lively and successful church; more dynamic and more successful than the one across town. This leads to pride, hardness, man-centredness and rivalry.

Paul writes in Galatians 5:25-26: *"Since we live by the Spirit, let us keep in step with the Spirit. Let us not become conceited, competing against one another, envying one another."*

It took me many years to see that the above two verses are part of an application designed to enable me to live out the implications of the fruit of the Spirit in every detail of my life. Stated quite simply, Paul reminds me that there is no place for spiritual pride. On the one hand I am, by God's grace, to produce the nine flavours of the fruit of the Spirit in my personal spiritual walk. On the other hand, the result of that is shown in how I keep in step with my brothers and sisters in Christ.

"Conceit" is a sentiment of feeling superior to others. *"Competition"* is an action of seeking to win. It is much like when my grandson Ajay and I *"pretend fight"* he always claims, *"I won."* Whereas a spiritual superiority complex declares, *"I am better than you and I will show you,"* a spiritual inferiority complex states, *"you are better than me and I resent it."* *"Envying one another"* results and that is as much pride as the others. When these sentiments are present in my heart, I fail to keep in step in the Spirit.

I remember a story told to me when a boy. Old monks met in their monastery every night to sing to the Lord, albeit with their croaky voices. One evening they were joined by a young monk who sang with a beautiful baritone voice. He sang alone that evening. Later, when the oldest monk knelt to pray, the Lord asked him why he did not sing to him earlier in the evening. He explained that he could not compete with the new monk. The Lord replied: *"I didn't hear anyone!"*

That is just a story but the lesson I am still learning is not to compare myself to others. Unless I stay connected to God, through Christ, my sense of value as a person will come from how I perform as a person and how others reward and applaud my behaviour. Right standing with God is through Christ. In him each of us is an original and we glory in each other.

The following list of positive and negative qualities of Christians are what I have observed in the lives of those in spiritual leadership. I call it a list of the *"do"* and *"do nots"* of pastoral care.

It is easy to know if someone cares and if they are worthy of trust. True pastors communicate that they care, and at that moment convey that no one is more important to them than the person they are helping. They listen and do not interrupt or pass judgement. There is no disdain. They do not arrive late for a rendezvous and then make lame excuses. Neither do they indicate that their time is limited to a few minutes, nor that they must meet someone else soon.

While making a list of statements like these, I acknowledge that it is not easy to give counsel or comfort, but there are simple ground rules that act as safeguards. Confidentialities are to be guarded and never mentioned to others. When a counsellor is out of his/her depth, for example, with those who suffer clinical depression, it is right and proper to indicate where proper help may be found elsewhere.

Christians ought to expect their share of buffetings in life. The road winds uphill to the very end. Sadly, there are preachers who teach there is an easy way to holiness, for example, an experience, a technique, or a blessing to lofty heights! These are recipes for disasters. We begin as spiritual babies and grow into adulthood.

As I look back through more than sixty years of experience as a professing Christian, I have been slow to realize that the first Christians ministered to the poor. All too often affluence leads Christians to arrogance and to feeling the right to special treatment. Yet Scripture emphasizes that the poor are targets of special love and that the spiritual fruits of poverty can be very great. All Christians are to hold the world's goods in trust for the needy. Helping the poor is not peripheral to the proclamation of good news in Jesus but central to it. Indeed, this compassion is an outflow of God's nature and proof of a work of grace.

There is another evidence of God's grace in our hearts as an index of spiritual health and well-being. Peter writes in 1 Peter 3:10: *"He that would love life and see good days, let him keep his tongue from evil and his lips from speaking guile."* The tongue is the master-key to it all. The holy life is a direct responsibility of each Christian, and at its heart is the tongue!!

Biblical holiness is evident in a down-to-earth life. This includes love for our neighbour demonstrated in care for the needy and deprived. Any profession of my faith which fails in love and compassion is not genuine. True Christian faith risks itself for the sake of those in danger. As a member of a church, I must fight against feelings that imperil fellowship and words that denigrate a brother. In everyday life, I am to discharge my debts, guard my reactions, pray for the needy and the sick, share with those who are distressed, and use every God-given opportunity to pursue gently and urgently those who need Jesus.

I cannot finish this chapter without including the blessing of true friendship. By that I mean a friend who speaks the truth when others tell you what you want to hear, someone who thinks you are great but does not always think you are right. The person who cares and respects your need to be alone yet understands your fear of being lonely. To whom can you share your highest hopes, your biggest dreams, or the very smallest corner of your world?

At times, if you are like me, you run ahead or lag; a true friend will be there with an outstretched hand each time you fall. I have two, or maybe three, companions who will never turn from me, run out on me, or give up on me. I am blessed by those who have remained true friends over the years. Yet, my truest friend is Jesus Christ, the Son of God.

A BIBLICAL PRAYER
(Ephesians 3:20-21)

Now all glory to God, who is able, through his mighty power at work within us, to accomplish infinitely more than we might ask and think. Glory to him in the church and in Christ Jesus through all generations forever and ever! Amen

I owe the title of this chapter to a Presbyterian minister who explained his eulogy to a bad-tempered church member as *"a work in progress."* I readily include myself in the analogy. After all, to profess to know God through Christ leaves little room for pride and to know myself leads me to acknowledge that I need to allow more of the Lord's grace to manifest itself in me.

Scripture outlines (1 Corinthians 8:2-3) the need for modesty when tempted to be a know-it-all: *"[2] Anyone who claims to know all the answers doesn't really know very much. [3] But the person who loves God is the one whom God recognizes."*

God enriches me with the grace of his presence when I obey his commands and seek him. The first element in the battle to stay near to God is the discipline of Bible reading, prayer, private and public worship, feasting at the Lord's Table, devoting myself to Christian fellowship, and cultivating every avenue whereby I can draw close to God.

Then there is the purification of self. This does not just happen because it requires obedience to the revealed Word of God. My desire is to clean up my conduct and my heart and to be like God. To do so I lament my sin and repent of it. The Lord sets the downward path before me because there is no other way to go up. The act of humbling myself before the Lord requires self-examination. The logs go out as I practise the presence of God. As always, the more I pursue his likeness, the more deeply and sorrowfully my sinfulness and shortcomings are exposed.

Allow me to illustrate the one area that convinces me personally. Defamatory, unloving speech issues from my heart when the love of Jesus is not present. Vilification of others begins and lives on in the mind. It is on the ground of undeserved mercy that both critic and criticized stand together as kin of the same Father. When I set myself up as better than someone else, and as judging a person I thus usurp the authority of God himself. God's law is an expression of who and what he is. To value my opinions above that is to value myself above him.

Who am I? A dreadful lack of self-knowledge lies behind every judgement passed on fellow-Christians! As indicated above, the way up is down, and the way down is the way up, where the hardest route to take is to actively seek the lowest place. Biblical images of the frailty of human life that looks like a vapour to God is a reminder that riches are uncertain, a futile goal, and that wealth leads many to presumption and to its misuse.

Familiarity can still breed contempt, and success conceit, as though the very gifts that bring prosperity were not gifts at all, and the patient love of God were weakness. Old Testament Scripture in Deuteronomy 7:7-8 outlines God's eternal love for his people: *"The Lord did not set his heart on you because you were more numerous than other nations, for you were the smallest of all nations. Rather, it was simply that the Lord loves you...."*

True spirituality is fellowship with God, and in relation to other people, is demonstrated by what I say about them. The ordering of my life and laying of plans begin in seeking guidance from God and are evident in my use of this world's resources and goods. This God-given wisdom cannot be enjoyed if my life is not being kept in a right relationship with God himself, whereby I am daily nourished by his grace.

There is no room for an expression of self-interest within the family of God. This biblical metaphor calls me to care for and love my neighbour, to guard my speech, and to foster good relationships. Bad relations and a divisive attitude towards others, show that the truth and my heart are strangers to each other.

Self-centred feelings are the issues! Christians rightly teach that peace with God has been achieved through Christ's atoning death on the cross. God's people are indwelt by the Spirit of God and there is no way that living in the presence of the Spirit is compatible with sinful yearnings and promptings to egotism which destroy the peace of the church and interrupt interpersonal relations.

Perhaps the greatest scandal among Christians remains a breakdown in relationships. I contribute to that disgrace when I denigrate, criticise, make sly innuendo comments about people who yet bear the image of God. I make a start towards a return to God by the way I speak to myself inwardly about or to someone else. The initial point is the image of God in the other person. This is the pathway to sanctification and to the final work of grace when I meet Jesus.

Why then do I consider myself to be a work in progress? Implicit in my focus is that there is always more to know and share. Scripture opens horizons of expectancy and broadens out all that God by his Spirit wants to do in us. There is both the possibility of reacting with extreme childish gullibility and of sceptical rationalism.

God is not served well when the spotlight is placed on what some regard as exceptional and extraordinary. On the other hand, it is equally silly to preclude any manifestation of the power and glory of God because we find it hard to explain and control events in life. When Paul writes to the Corinthian church, he concentrates on what they reckon to be the more dramatic gifts, he finds them in disorder, heresy, immorality, and division.

God transcends our finite minds, and he reveals himself unexpectantly in our mortal existence. I will always thank him for the supreme miracle that happens in conversion and regeneration but have come to expect him to work out further miracles in my life thereafter. Spiritual growth is therefore a process and not a plateau.

Until Jesus comes again, I have a sure foundation for my expectant faith. Those who are Christ's will be gathered into his presence and transformed into unblemished holiness. To believers Jesus' coming is a sure hope, a call to endure, and to prepare by holiness of life. The wonder of the day of Jesus' coming is that the full content of God's heart of love will come home in experience to all who love God.

The doctrine of the Christian life is a process of growth towards holiness, like a harvest. Our tongues can disrupt and rob us of the yield. The crop comes as we enjoy the *"soil"* of Christian fellowship. My part to play is to watch my heart just as Jesus did when he set his face to Jerusalem to do God's will. In the same way my heart lies at the centre of my lifestyle. God looks for a heart fixed now on the anticipation of eternal fellowship in heaven.

The older I get the more I can look back with heartfelt thanks for the benefits reaped through experiences which at the time were full of grief and pain. God decided to provide for me a purity I could never attain on my own. That is why he gave his Son, Jesus Christ, to die for us all on the cross. It is only when my sins have been washed in the blood of Christ that I appear as white as snow in the eyes of God. No human *"detergent"* of good works or clean thoughts can make me that white, that pure. Only Christ's precious blood can do that, and it is only his blood that can continue to cleanse me from sin.

Salvation by faith alone is recognized by the fruit. I, like all God's people, am redeemed by the blood of Christ but not yet home. My faith is tried to test its genuineness, and the task is unremitting. To this there is an aim because the path is of testing, endurance, and perseverance and leads me to reform my thinking in the light of God's Word. Do I know anything that my heart wants more than to be made like the Son of God in all things?

At the judgement seat of Christ I, like every child of God, will give an account of having been given salvation, the indwelling Spirit, the Scriptures, the gospel message, and so much more. I am to be in a constant state of readiness as I examine my own heart and life to see whether I am prepared to stand before the Lord without shame and to his praise, glory, and pleasure. He will see to it then that I am no longer a work in progress.

The Apostle Paul sums up his experience of following Christ in his letter to the Philippian church (3:9, 10, 12-14):

> *[9] I no longer count on my own righteousness through obeying the law; rather, I become righteous through faith in Christ. For God's way of making us right with himself depends on faith. [10] I want to know Christ and experience the mighty power that raised him from the dead.... [12] I don't mean to say that I have already achieved these things or that I have already reached perfection. But I press on to possess that perfection for which Christ Jesus first possessed me. [13] No dear brothers and sisters, I have not achieved it, but I focus on this one thing. Forgetting the past and looking forward to what lies ahead, [14] I press on to reach the end of the race and receive the heavenly prize for which God, through Christ Jesus, is calling us.*

When I think of all this, I fall to my knees and pray to the Father, the Creator of everything in heaven and on earth. I pray that from his glorious, unlimited resources he will empower you with inner strength through his Spirit. Then Christ will make his home in your hearts as you trust in him. Your roots will grow down into God's love and keep you strong. And may you have the power to understand, as all God's people should, how wide, how long, how high, and how deep his love is. May you experience the love of Christ, though it is too great to understand fully. Then you will be made complete with all the fulness of life and power that comes from God. Amen